CW01676683

lemon drizzle cake

& other fruit of the spirit

Yann Dubreuil and Alex Pease

Yann Dubreuil is French (although he says you wouldn't know it unless the rugby is on). He has had a wide and varied career. His professional background includes: unemployed actor; the world of insurance; teaching French in North East London; driving a van; children and youth worker. He is now the rector of Bentley, Froyle and Binsted Parish. He hates writing and has a deep distrust of those who enjoy it! He was formerly head of Rural Ministry for New Wine and now is on the national Fresh Expressions Rural Guiding Team.

Alex Pease is English (no-one would suspect him of being anything else). His professional background was as a territorial army soldier in the Royal Green Jackets for six years, as a solicitor (he worked at Allen & Overy LLP in London, Dubai and Tokyo) for 25 years. He has had 18 years experience of rural ministry (and has made every mistake in the book), taking the role of churchwarden, PCC secretary and PCC treasurer. He then acted as ordinand-in-training in the Upper Itchen Benefice, followed by five years as self-supporting curate and then assistant priest in Itchen Valley Parish. His current role is as rector of Itchen Valley Parish. Alex enjoys writing. He says it has been a lot of fun working with Yann!

In memory of

Revd. Bob Earnshaw 1942-2018

A rural evangelist before his time.

Published 2020

A CIP catalogue record for this book is available from the British Library

ISBN: 978-1-5272-5620-0

FSC www.fsc.org MIX Paper from responsible sources FSC® C108111

CONTENTS

Chapters

Thank you

We have so many people to thank for their openness and willingness to contribute to, and to critique, this book in its draft stages. A particular thank you to Yann's and Alex's friends and parishioners and Alex's friends in The Stewards Trust, many of whom live in rural parishes and have made so many useful contributions, in particular: Revd. James Campbell, Revd. David Cook, Ven. Robin King, Revd. Mary Cantacuzene, Revd. Christopher and Kathy Ogilvie-Thompson, Revd. Chris Dudgeon, Ruth Guy, Henry and Caroline Pomeroy and Phoebe Cameron, and Alex's friends from Winchester Diocese: Ven. Richard Brand, Colin Harbidge, Revd. Andrew Micklefield, Bruce Newson, Tessa Feilden, Beccy Clark and Sarah Shirley. Also great thanks to all the wonderful people who kindly contributed their testimonies of becoming followers of Christ and which are featured in the Appendix. Thank you also to Penny Russell for arranging all the publishing. Thanks to our wives Hannah and Lucy for putting up with us spending time on writing the book and to Lucy for her help in proof reading. Also, a particular thank you to Revd. Bob Earnshaw, who sadly died just before receiving a final draft of this book and to whom this book is dedicated.

Yann and Alex, December 2019

CHAPTER ONE

Introduction

Lemon Drizzle Cake. It's delicious and such a staple of country fetes and English garden tea parties, that it is almost a national institution. But for the rural minister, who has the sensitivity to see the work of the Holy Spirit in the everyday, in the ordinary, in what is present, a kind word to the cook can invest in the making of something as routine as cake, a sense of such significance, that a new ministry is born.

This is just one of the ideas which we explore below, for the intended readers of this book who are New Wine ministers who have just taken on (or are about to take on) a rural benefice, when they have little or no experience of this form of mission and who come from a lively church in a city or a suburb. We also hope that this book will help to encourage those who might otherwise rule out a rural benefice, to think again.

The rural church is different to the city or suburban church. It can seem an upside-down world and is full of traps for the unwary, particularly New Wine ministers who come from such a different environment. We also aim to point out some of these traps and to help ministers avoid making mistakes and trashing their new ministry in the first one or two weeks of their arrival! People have long memories in the countryside. It's easy to wreck things right at the beginning.

This is a practical book. We are not writing a theology of the rural church. It is based on the simple assumption that the role of any church is to love God, love neighbour and crucially to make disciples.

We start by looking at the place that rural church takes in the vast range of Christian worship throughout the UK, on the basis of the statistical evidence that we can gather. We hope that this will set aside some prejudices in the minds of those who have worked entirely in cities or suburbs about the contribution that the rural church can make to the national church.

We will also be looking at the less tangible, the more anecdotal, what we have learned from our own experience and interviews we have conducted with others. We will be seeing how we don't need (and generally should not try) to import to the countryside all the methods of a New Wine church in a suburb or a city. But we will see how by adding God to the traditional, to the naturally occurring community events (even the making of lemon drizzle cake), they can be claimed for Christ and have a profound effect. We will also be seeing how we need to challenge the status quo in the rural church and in particular, we will be seeking to explore the territory between being a churchgoer and becoming a disciple of Christ.

The rural church is a wonderful opportunity for the gospel and can be a very agreeable place to serve and can make a great contribution to the villages in which it is set. As Archdeacon Robin King writes: 'A rural church can be missional, (knowing people, building relationships, having time and the chance to make good contacts with non-church people), incarnational (belonging, being cared for as well as caring for), environmental (fresh air, bird song, noticing the rhythm of the seasons, beauty), social (being connected and involved, being asked in by non-church folk, the expectation that you will make friends), relational, educational, physical, mental – to say nothing of the cake!' But it's best not to arrive with major misconceptions. Let's get one thing absolutely clear: rural ministry is not, on the whole, about farming! The number of people involved in agriculture in a rural community given the massive development of the tractor in the last 50 years, is now tiny. In a rural parish you are likely to have more accountants, school teachers, bricklayers, decorators and gardeners, than farmers.

Of course, every rural parish is different. You have the 'deep rural' beyond commuter distance from a major city, where the agricultural will still dominate, and then the 'commuter rural' of the sort of churches where Yann and Alex serve. They have their different challenges. What we also tend to mean by 'rural', is churches set in villages or groups of villages with a total population of no more than 2000 people. But whether deep rural or commuter rural, the church can be the centre of many community activities where large numbers of people, who would not normally regard themselves as worshippers, can be drawn to attend.

We should also point out that the villages in which we, the authors, have experience are in Hampshire and we are drawing our anecdotes and stories from our own experience in those villages and from the experience of those we have interviewed (who come from a slightly broader geography). We recognise that not everything we say will be applicable to rural churches in, say, Northumberland, but we can only speak to our own experience and hope that what we say will resonate in some areas with those who have had a different sort of experience of rural church.

Perhaps our most important conclusion is that the key test of a church, of mission in a community, is not whether the church building is full at Christmas and Easter (many rural churches in England, particularly in commuter rural areas, are) but whether individuals are coming to faith in Jesus Christ in these places: whether people would say that their real journey of faith as a follower[1] of Jesus Christ began in that rural church. Are those who attend consumers or followers

1. The Alpha International Annual Review 2016 notes that after Alpha 82% of non-Christians described themselves as 'followers of Jesus'. The review continues: 'Although becoming a follower of Jesus does not necessarily equate to conversion to Christianity, a variety of data points demonstrate significant spiritual impact and even radical change of life among the 82% of non-Christians who described themselves as followers of Jesus since doing Alpha'. Asking the question how many 'reborn' or 'converted' people you have in a church might be seen to exclude those committed Christians from the contemplative tradition, as this language tends not to be used outside evangelical circles. So, we have chosen to seek to distinguish between 'consumers' of Jesus (those who attend church but belief in Jesus does not significantly affect their life decisions) and 'followers' of Jesus (those who attend church and for whom seeking to be his disciple is the most significant or a very significant part of their lives.

of Jesus Christ? We look at this issue in Chapter 3: Making Followers.

A typical difference of most rural churches to those that pastors or members of New Wine or HTB churches will have experienced is the theological approach or churchmanship of the church. As Revd. James Campbell says: 'The default position of many rural Church of England parishes is "middle Anglican" with a strong desire to avoid confrontation and any perceived form of extremism'. But, actually, the relationship between the wings of the church is more of a triangle – Catholic/Evangelical/Liberal - and not a continuum with Liberal in the reasonable middle! As one rural Rector on the Catholic wing of the Church of England said to Alex during his ordination training (when he was looking round churches in Winchester Diocese): 'Please don't think of me as a liberal…I know 'liberal catholic' trips off the tongue, but that is not what I am!' Professor Leslie Francis sees the relationship between the different wings of the church as two separate scales – one with conservative and liberal at the different ends and another with catholic and evangelical at different ends[2]. Whichever way you look at it, liberalism is not the reasonable middle between catholic and evangelical.

However, highlighting the differences between churchmanships to church members is probably just going to annoy those who would not otherwise have

2. *Rural Theology* Volume 16, May 2018 page 36 as quoted by C.J.F Rutledge

recognized that the differences exist. They may well, however, have a view on what they will call 'happy-clappy' churches. Alex tends to say in response to being called a 'happy-clappy' or told that this or that church is 'happy-clappy', 'don't you think that being happy is a good thing?'

The objection is really to a caricature of inane worship (the couple singing 'Kumbaya' in the movie Four Weddings and a Funeral for example) which is so far removed from the sort of worship that HTB or any New Wine church will engage in, that it has to be seen as meaning 'Don't treat us as if we are stupid'. There is a snobbish social comment underlying this, which is really a country vs suburban thing, which one needs to be conscious about, but perhaps not give too much air time to. Holy Trinity Brompton's approach of not talking about different styles of churchmanship (and seeing what we can learn from them all, because all are valuable) is a very good one for the rural church. Of course, these days many of us are rather more mixed in our own churchmanship than perhaps we used to be. Our prejudices in this area may not be based on theological difference, but, rather, actually on personality difference; people who prefer quiet to noise; introverts in comparison with extroverts. It may be better to address this by not highlighting differences, but by explaining why the church has got to the stage that it has reached. A lot of work on this issue of personality type and its impact on churches in the UK has been done by Leslie Francis. Having a focus on theological conviction rather than style can help us to address such challenges.

In any event, we need to remember that our rural church is (probably) the only show in town in our communities; there are unlikely to be churches of other denominations, except in the nearby city. We have to be able to appeal to a wide range of churchmanship. We need to be able to do a good job of leading Book of Common Prayer communions at 8am, Evensong at 6pm and even Matins at 11am, however unfamiliar they may be to us, if they are reasonably well attended. Some have been delighted and astonished to return to Cranmer's words since encountering them in childhood, they are so theologically robust! In any event, we cannot take the view 'Well, if they don't like what we are doing in the church, they can always go elsewhere', because they cannot; this is their church, the church in their community; it's not unreasonable that we lead services which suit them. If parishioners do leave the church over the sort of services which we are conducting, then they remain in the community, probably saying very negative things about our leadership of the church. They don't just disappear, as they might in a city!

But how do we do these BCP services well, if we are unfamiliar with them? It's simple. We ask. Alex found that asking one of the key supporters of Evensong to comment on how he had led that service helped enormously. He said, 'Don't announce each section; just let it flow. All of us who attend know the words backwards'. James Campbell writes, 'Those familiar with [these services] love for [them] to flow unannounced. However, if I ever see anyone in the congregation who doesn't know their way around, I will do page numbers unless it's totally obvious. It's so easy to alienate visitors'.

On the whole, the Evensong congregation in Itchen Valley would prefer a short contemplative homily to a full preach, but that may not be practicable (as preparing two sermons a week may be too demanding) and in any event one wants to keep the evening congregation in touch with what the rest of the parish has heard that Sunday. Be brave with these services. Sing the responses, there are only three notes to master, and if Alex can do this, with his very limited vocal range, anyone can!

Of course, these 1662 services will not suit everyone, particularly those under 60 who may not be familiar with them. They are unlikely to be the foundation stone of a church which is growing in numbers in the twenty first century. But what sort of services should we be leading if we want a growing church in the countryside? We explore some options in Chapter Eight.

The biggest problem of leading a rural church is that it is such a full-time job for the Rector just keeping the whole show on the road. A very big difficulty can be the multiplicity of villages and churches in a rural benefice, particularly if each village has its own parish. One vicar who had spent 6 years working in a group of six parishes could find only five advantages of a multi parish benefice (as opposed to a multi church parish) and 15 disadvantages!

If we are appointed as the Rector of a rural church, we will almost certainly have at least four churches for which we are responsible. These may come with four PCCs. Alex's church during his ordination training had six churches, six PCCs, 12 churchwardens, six treasurers, six PCC secretaries, six Safeguarding Officers, six Health and Safety officers and 12 Deanery Synod Representatives; in all at least 48 officers and there were a number of additional PCC members as well. This was for a total church population of about 200. So, if we assume that a family is four people, we had about one church officer for every family who attended! The danger with this is that the PCC becomes the tool of personal preference of individual families (or even individual people) rather than a means of determining the wishes and needs of the community. The poor Rector is spinning so many plates that it is difficult for her to turn to mission or to innovation, quite apart from managing six power bases all of which will have different objections to any of her proposals. The delay in getting consent from each body which wants to be asked can stifle any initiative.

Itchen Valley Parish, where Alex is now serving as

Rector, took the brave step of merging its four parishes into one a few years ago. Although this is not without its challenges, it is a huge advantage over a multi parish benefice from the perspective of the Rector. However, it is a major exercise to get agreed and can be very bruising for all involved. We cover this process in detail in Chapter 12 and look at the advantages and disadvantages of merging parishes.

Change will undoubtedly be necessary. But expect that it will take time, particularly in a conservative rural parish. James Campbell writes 'Even in Bentley we slowly moved from a half hour morning service at 9.30am plus Matins at 11am to an informal service once a month and it took 10 years for a worship leader to answer our prayers'.

CHAPTER TWO

The Lie of the Land

But why bother with the rural church at all, you may be thinking? Surely all our effort should be going into churches in the cities and suburbs?

From the perspective of the bustling importance of a city with its huge population and desperate social problems, it is easy to imagine that churches in rural areas are of little significance. But a few numbers draw attention to the national importance of the rural church.

10.4 percent of Britain's population live in settlements of 1000 or less. If we are to ignore that 10%, it is the equivalent of ignoring a population twice the size of Birmingham, Leeds, Newcastle, Liverpool, and Manchester put together. No-one would have a national strategy which ignored these six cities.

In addition to that 10 per cent, 1.4 per cent of Britain's population live in villages with populations of between 1000 and 2000 and about 5 per cent live in villages or country towns of up to 5000. So rural deaneries which centre on county towns surrounded by tiny villages represent a very considerable 16% of the UK population or over 10 million people – more than the combined population of Scotland and Wales.

It's not surprising to read that the rural church makes up 'two thirds of Church of England parishes and 40% of the worshippers'.[3]

However, despite this, there does appear to be a general narrative abroad that there is a disproportionate number of Church of England stipendiary ministers in the rural church in comparison with the suburban and urban church. It has been said that there is a huge disparity (1 in 1500 in rural churches in comparison with 1 in 24000 in urban areas). But this does not take into account the much larger distribution of other Christian denominations in suburban and urban areas. It is difficult to get good data to assess the situation, but the impression that we have, (having researched it in some detail and making calculations for the northern half of Winchester Diocese) taking into account those other denominations, is that the disparity is not nearly so high; indeed, there may not be a disparity at all! This whole area is dogged by a lack of accurate data. Even the distinction between urban, suburban and rural parishes appears difficult to make, as some of the data which is periodically referred to relies upon 'self-referential' categorisations of what is an urban/suburban/rural church rather than clear categories dependent upon, say, civil population figures. This would not matter too much if it were not for the fact

3. Strategies for Growth, p2

that we are reaching an age where decision making on clergy deployment is being made relying upon these distinctions and a perceived impression that urban areas are worse for the deployment of ministers per head of population in comparison with rural areas, whereas in fact the situation may not be all that different, taking into account the other denominations. It is difficult to see why one would not take those other denominations into account when planning clergy deployment, as after all Anglicanism does not have a monopoly on Christian truth and, surely, ecumenical cooperation must be the way of the future.

It's not just the huge numbers of people involved. When it comes to raising money for the church, the potential of the rural church is significant. In Winchester Diocese the money requested per worshipping community member in a rural deanery (on average £515 per Worshipping Community Member) is greater than the money requested in urban deaneries (£367) and deaneries with a mix of rural and urban parishes (£463). This happens in Winchester Diocese because, the amount requested for each worshipping community member is affluence adjusted to reflect (based on independent calculations) the ability of a community to pay. However, it should be pointed out that the amount requested does not always get paid! Also, the prevailing narrative is that rural richer Deaneries are less generous on a per head per week committed giving basis, but again the figures (as they are based on blunt average contributions per head), could be misleading where there are one or two very generous donors (thus lifting the figures) or many donors giving tiny amounts who, were they living in an urban context, might not give at all.

Even so, the combined contribution of all the rural deaneries is more or less equal to the combined contribution of all the urban deaneries, at just under £3,000,000 per annum[4]. The rural deaneries have 37 clergy between them, the city and suburban mixed deaneries 49 and the city deaneries almost 60. Whilst every deanery is likely to have a mix of urban, suburban and rural parishes which will skew this analysis somewhat, it is clear that, as a whole, the rural church is at least self-funding but has the potential to be a huge financial support to urban ministry, rather than the other way round. If we were to allow the rural church to slide off into decline, it could easily lead to economic disaster for the whole Church of England. This is of course because some of the most-wealthy live in our idyllic rural communities.

The impact of the church on the secular population is greater in the rural church than in the urban church. This can be seen by the huge numbers of people attending church at Christmas and Easter in rural benefices where the church is still central to the community. The Diocese with the most effective

4. Figures extracted from *Winchester Diocesan Clergy Deployment Seminar* 10th June 2019

penetration in terms of attendance per head of population is Hereford – an almost entirely rural Diocese. Shaping Strategies for Growth observes: 'The larger the population of the parish the smaller the proportion of that population the church is in touch with.'[5]. 'It is the knowing and being known that goes with smaller populations and indeed congregations that is valuable'.

The worshipping community as a percentage of the total civil population in Winchester Diocese is 4.3% in predominantly rural deaneries, in comparison with 2.3% in mixed rural and urban deaneries and 1.2% in urban areas. Also, the number of Worshipping Community Members in rural deaneries per clergyperson is 153, in mixed rural and city, 167 and in City Deaneries 132.

So far as growth is concerned, it might be assumed that rural churches are in decline and urban churches are growing, but in fact 18% of all churches (whether rural or urban) are growing. Whether a church is growing or not does not seem to depend at all on whether the church is rural or urban.

The rural church is significant. It is a suitable place for New Wine priests to work. We can lead people to become followers of Jesus Christ. But there are traps for the unwary and we will be dealing with these next.

5. Op. cit. page 9

CHAPTER THREE

Making Followers

Our Lord calls us to 'love God, love neighbour and make disciples' – two great commands and one great commission. It's not one or another. It's not just the second one – important as that is – it is all three. But the acid test of rural ministry is surely the third: whether we (in partnership with the Holy Spirit) make disciples. We will need to do not only the sowing (our preaching and other things we do to broadcast the Word) but also the reaping (our leading to discipleship of those whose hearts have been changed). The Holy Spirit does the mysterious bit in between, as Jesus explains to us in the parable of the growing seed (Mark 6:23-24). But in all of this, the ultimate aim of work in the rural church should be the Great Commission – making disciples. If we are making real disciples, real followers of Christ, then they will love God and love neighbour – this will just naturally flow from them.

Robin King writes: 'I saw a great film recently called *Founder*. It was about a chap called Ray Kroc who was selling ice-cream machines in the mid-fifties when he met Richard and Maurice McDonald who ran a hamburger bar in California. Shortly after Ray Kroc got involved with the company, he was struggling to make any money at all and was eventually saved by a business man who pointed out that he had not understood what the business was all about. Ray Kroc assumed he was working in the restaurant business when in fact he was in the property business. McDonald's built its empire on the money from the rent paid by the franchisees, not from the actual selling of burgers. We do indeed need to remember/understand what it is we're about or we will become exhausted with little to show for our efforts'.

Reiterating that we are in the business of making disciples, making followers of Christ, is all the more important because of the findings of a recent Church of England study entitled Released for Mission: growing the rural church, indicate that one of the characteristics of a growing church in rural areas is 'An intentional focus on mission and evangelism, beyond a focus on Sunday worship[6]'.

When it is so difficult to bring people into a relationship with Jesus in the countryside, it is easy to change our focus to another direction. As Revd. Sally Gaze says in her excellent book Mission Shaped and Rural (using the analogy of farming), 'When being fruitful is hard, it is easier to find some sort of sense of achievement by changing the focus away from harvest to keeping the 'farms' going'[7]. But Jesus tells us that

6. As quoted in 2017 paper by the Church of England entitled: *Shaping strategies for mission and growth in rural multi church groups* p.5 https://www.churchofengland.org

7. *Mission Shaped and Rural* by Revd. Sally Gaze page 3

bearing fruit is the name of the game: John 15:16 'You did not choose me, but I chose you and appointed you so that you might go and bear fruit – fruit that will last.' Ultimately whether a rural church is doing something useful or not (except the very low-level aim of just of keeping the show on the road for another generation) is: has anyone recently become a follower of Christ in that parish? Robin King writes: 'People always say to me that it's not just about bums on pews. When I ask them if they'd prefer their congregation to halve or to double, it soon becomes apparent that bums do matter!'

By 'follower of Christ' we mean someone for whom Christ's teaching, as expressed in the Bible, is the most important factor in their life decisions. Everything flows from this. If we have people regularly becoming followers of Christ in the rural church, then we will have no problem finding volunteers being willing to prioritize their time for outreach of various kinds to build the Kingdom and change the world and we will have no problem meeting (and even exceeding) our contribution to the Diocesan Common Mission Fund to support other churches in doing so.

Now we may argue that 'This is a long-term game' and 'We cannot be expected to make much progress in less than five years, ten years etc'. But we think one example suggests that this can in fact happen really quite fast: the life changing experience of becoming a follower of Jesus Christ in a few people's lives in a rural church came at a personal cost to one new Rector himself. Revd. Bob Earnshaw was the Rector of a multi church benefice in Hampshire in the 1980s. By his own admission he was rather 'zealous' in those early days, possibly more so than he might have been later in his ministry. His encounter with Tessa (described in the Appendix) gives a window on the sort of conversations that he had with some of his parishioners. It was early days for evangelicals in the rural church and some of the parishioners felt that his approach was not appropriate for a country parish and let the Bishop know their views! He was Rector for around only two years before he felt he should leave. Reading the (normally anodyne) minutes of the PCC meetings during this time, one can sense the withering criticism to which he was subjected for wanting to 'grow the church'. But Bob was a man who was way ahead of his time. During those few months that he was in the benefice, at least three people came to faith in Jesus Christ who have gone on to have a lasting impact on that community and elsewhere.

It's true (and is often said) that 'You cannot see what is going on under the surface' and, of course, we don't know how effective a church is being by just looking at the surface and we believe that God is at work wherever we are, however dead it seems. Indeed, when Elijah complained to God in 1 Kings 18:14 that 'I am the only one [worshipping Yahweh] left', God replied 'I reserve 7000 in Israel all whose knees have not bowed down to Baal and whose mouths have not kissed him'. If Elijah could not spot the disciples who surrounded him then, probably, we will not be able to do so either. We will not necessarily see what is going on in the hearts of those around us.

Also, there is no doubt that within a parish there are people at different stages of their spiritual journeys. It is so important to spend time with everyone, regardless of the stage they have reached. Every conversation brings us closer to becoming the person to whom they may turn in a crisis, when their self-sufficiency has run out, so that we can lead them to Christ. We can and should see everyone in the parish population as a person with whom we are developing a relationship which may lead them to become a follower of Christ. We are, after all, His ambassador in these communities.

However, when we see no change in any particular individual's life or priorities on the surface, no fruit, then, although it is possible that something is going on 'under the surface', we must accept that there is at least the possibility that there has been no change under the surface either and the spiritual journey has not actually begun or has run into a cul-de-sac. We need to be realistic about this. It is very easy to be seduced as a Rector into putting on more and more church events in a community, which lead nowhere in terms of followership. The villagers love any kind of local entertainment. But we need to be hard headed, as much as we are soft-hearted. Is what we are spending our time doing potentially leading to people coming to faith or not? Do we have a means of picking up those on the cusp of faith and leading them gently into becoming disciples? If not, then why are we there? And, of course, when we do lead someone to faith, it is so exciting (partly because on the whole it does not happen all the time in the rural church) that it compensates for all the everyday administration which can occupy a lot of our lives as rural church leaders!

What changes are we looking for, to see if someone has become a follower of Christ? This is a very difficult question and requires spiritual discernment. Almost certainly we will not always get this right and, of course, we can feel that we are being judgemental, even if we never reveal our conclusions to others, which obviously we should not. But we are not actually seeking to 'judge' whether someone will be saved or condemned, final judgment is God the Father's role and to do so would be an attempt by us to limit his mercy. We should never think that simply because someone has not become a follower of Christ at any particular time means that they never will. Difficult as this is, we do need to exercise our discernment as to where someone is on the spiritual journey so that we can help them onto the next stage, even if this means sometimes calling out sinful behaviour in them.

Naturally, the Bible helps us in this discernment process. We should expect to see in an individual's life the fruit of the spirit as shown in Galatians 5: love, joy, peace, forbearance, kindness, goodness, faithfulness, gentleness and self-control. Followers of Christ hear his voice and respond by seeking out the Shepherd. Does the object of our discernment appear to recognise Jesus voice – John 10.27? Are they responsive to His call? Is this something that they will speak about to us? We need to be alert to these intimations of His guidance. This is not about a grasp of theology; quite often disciples start following Jesus before they have entirely got the vision of who He is.

Asking the question 'How can you discern where people are on their spiritual journey?' reminds us rather of the question asked of Jesus by John the Baptist from gaol: 'Are you the Messiah?' Jesus' response was 'Look around and describe what you see'. It's a bit like that. What sort of questions are they asking? Do they show a wish to follow Jesus' teaching? Are they attending a home group? How are they engaging with others? Do they have open hearts to hear the gospel? We look around at everything that the individual concerned is saying and doing. One indicator of followership might include, when they hear the word 'Jesus' on the radio, whether they turn it up or turn it off…?

So, it's difficult, it requires discernment, to know whether someone has come into a discipleship relationship with Jesus. And equally, as we are working in partnership with the Holy Spirit and we never know who He is likely to bring to faith, because, as Jesus points out to Nicodemus in John 3:8 'The wind blows where it chooses, and you hear the sound of it, but you do not know where it comes from or where it goes. So, it is with everyone who is born of the Spirit', we need to be engaging with as broad a sweep of people in the community as we can. If we are to see everyone in the parish population as a potential follower of Christ then we need to put on services or events which will attract a range of different people, rather than just lots of local entertainment for the same people.

It is for this reason that we might be willing (for example) to put on some kind of service which commemorates those who have died (whether you call it an All Souls Service or not and making any necessary adjustments so that the liturgy is consistent with our theology) for the benefit of those who have been bereaved in previous years, as this may bring us into contact with a different group of people to those who attend our other services and events. In one parish the church puts on a Thanksgiving Service in December to which the bereaved are invited, in which candles are lit to commemorate the names of those who have died and silver stars are inscribed with their names, which subsequently are used to decorate the Christmas tree in the church.

Alex also sees Itchen Valley Parish's annual Way of the Cross which is an Easter pageant in which the story of the Passion is acted out by adults ending up in one of the churches of the Parish and Carols in the Barn, which is a tableau of the nativity story in a barn with live sheep and other animals, if we can get them, as ways of involving and getting to know those (particularly men) on the periphery of the Church. Yann also sees in Bentley, Froyle and Binsted the potential in services like the traditional pet service. Bringing God into the traditional and naturally occurring events in rural church will be a major theme in this book. We cover various approaches to evangelism in the rural church in Chapter Six and differing approaches to services in Chapter Eight.

In His wonderful way, the Holy Spirit just acts where He chooses to act in our communities, not where we have planned for Him to go! We need to be constantly on the look-out for what God is doing and, in Archbishop Rowan's words, seek to join in.

It was thought a good idea to conduct interviews with as many rural parishioners who would describe themselves as followers of Christ and who had become so in the rural church and discover the circumstances in which this occurred and interview those in the ministry team who were around at the time – their stories are set out in the Appendix and help to inform the conclusions we have reached in various sections of this book.

However, we don't have to evaluate a church by the number of people who are becoming followers of Christ. Alex recently realized that the parable of the sower in Matthew 13 has only four categories, not five: the path (where the message is snatched away), rocky ground (where the message has no root and doesn't stick), thorns (where the message is throttled by worries and the deceitfulness of wealth) and good soil (where the message brings forth a hundred, sixty or thirty times what was sown). There isn't a category for where the sower sows seeds and only one or two true disciples are produced! If any true disciples are made in a parish through what we are doing during our tenure as Rector, then we can be optimistic that the Lord will bring a hundred, sixty or thirty times in due course. It so often feels as if we are sowing on hard ground, that the brief experiences that we have of people being drawn to Jesus and becoming genuine disciples can be very encouraging looked at from this perspective. They are first fruits.

A further question to ask, when we don't see any fruit, is 'Have I been faithful?'. The tree strains towards the water, rather than worrying too much about its fruit. This can be very encouraging in what can be rather bleak days of continued prayer and hard work, but seeing nothing happen. But we should expect to see glimpses of God at work. These signs will make a difference to our morale. Sometimes we may see these glimpses when we have already given up all hope of change. There is also a danger of missing the signs because we are looking for the wrong kind of results: signs of becoming a follower of Christ which would be usual in an urban or suburban context, but which may be different in a rural context. However, if we see nothing at all, then perhaps we need to consider and pray about whether the doors are closed, the ground is just too hard for us, the work has become a complete drudge and it is time to move on. There could well be a time when we shake the dust off our feet and go elsewhere.

CHAPTER FOUR

Starting Well - The new Rector

Imagine a packed theatre – with perhaps 2000 people (the entire population of a rural community) eagerly anticipating the beginning of the play. The lights come up and onto the stage walks a newly appointed Rector. One by one, or in groups, each member of the community steps onto the stage and greets the new Rector and has a conversation. The audience watch with rapt attention. We see him leading services with groups of people. We see him conducting funerals and weddings. We see good days and bad days. We overhear his telephone conversations and all his emails are projected onto a large screen for everyone to read. Whatever he says is exaggerated to make a good story. We see how he responds to rudeness, aggression, selfishness, unreasonable demands and condescension – but somehow it is only what he says, how he reacts which matters to the audience–the audience know the person that he is speaking to – she is one of their neighbours after all – and accept that is 'just them'. But everything that the new Rector says and does are seen and commented upon by the whole audience. At the end of the performance, there is either rapturous applause or the audience walk silently from the theatre muttering.

It shouldn't be the case. It's not fair. But whether a new Rector is popular in the community (perhaps 'favoured' by the community is a better expression) or not, is very, very important. It is through that favour, through the relationship between priest and person, through that friendship, that God will be introduced to unbelievers and the Holy Spirit may choose to begin a process by which they become disciples. It can be a long process. It can take many, many, conversations before a key moment of decision arises. But in the interim, the show has to be kept on the road. Favour plays a big role in ensuring that this can happen. Why? Well, we have to understand the motivations of the people who attend our church.

Understanding the motivations of our people

The motivations of Villagers One of the principal differences between city and suburban churches on the one hand and rural churches on the other is that the motivations of those attending church in the countryside are often completely different from those in the city or suburbs. Indeed, many of those who attend rural churches might not attend church at all if they were living in a city. In much of the countryside there is still a tradition of supporting the Rector. It can fall in the same category as 'doing our bit for the village'. The village into which we have poured our life savings, when we bought our house, or in which we grew up. The village in which we brought up our children. The character of the village in which we live, matters. It matters partly because it has an impact on the value of our property, but, more importantly, it matters because we want to spend the rest of our life living there and even to be buried there. The church is often one of the hubs of community activity. It is not the only one – the village hall, cricket club, pubs, village shop and primary school also help to build the character of the community, if the village is lucky enough to have any of them. But the church helps as well, particularly at Christmas and Easter and on important occasions like weddings, baptisms and funerals.

So, on the whole, villagers may well be disposed to be helpful to the church. They should be willing to contribute to work which needs to be done on the church building – even if they do not want to support the church as such – and this accounts for the success of the various 'Friends of St. Bartholomew's' which stand outside the legal structure of the church itself, are not run by the PCC, but are hugely helpful in covering the cost of maintaining the fabric of the buildings – see Chapter 11 below.

Villagers might, in addition to supporting the fabric of the church building, at a stretch, be willing to open up the church and toll the bell for services. Those with more Christian backgrounds (often those thoroughly immersed in Christian worship at school) might be willing to act as lesson and prayer readers, sides-men, churchwardens and PCC members. They might even be willing to attend services when the travelling show which is the rural church comes to their own particular village. They might even attend regularly. But, at the same time, they might have revealed to the Rector that they only have a very tentative belief in God, if at all. Their beliefs can include Deism (the belief that there is a God, but he is either not interested in or cannot affect our daily lives) but will often range from Agnosticism all the way through to actual Atheism. One newly appointed Rector was discussing with the choirmaster of the church choir how the music during their services should be about 'worship and not performance' and was astonished to hear the reply 'Worship what?'

Sometimes villagers indicate that they 'strongly support Christian values'. Sometimes they appreciate the church's role in being at the heart of the community. But many actually attend (particularly the elderly) for the social engagement with their neighbours. It's the coffee and biscuits after the service which they really care about, not necessarily the worship and almost certainly not the sermon! Alex has experienced one older parishioner who taps his watch during the preach – and mentions afterwards that any preaching should be done within 10 minutes 'If you cannot get your message across in ten minutes, then it's not worth saying at all…' Alex tends to reply 'There is no such thing as a sermon which is too long – just a bad sermon, I will try better next time'.

Villagers might even be willing (if they have the resources) to make regular contributions to the church so that the Common Mission Fund can be paid. It's important to remember that these are (almost always) really lovely people. They are often kind and look after their neighbours well, they are disposed to encourage the Rector and keep the show on the road. They would however probably not describe themselves as 'followers of Christ' or as 'disciples' (but would see themselves as 'Christians') and tend to see too much enthusiasm for Jesus as a bad thing. Indeed, one of the churches in Alex's parish has a tombstone to the Marchioness of Carnarvon who died in her thirties in the eighteenth century. Amongst her many virtues she is described, by her clearly distraught husband, as 'religious without enthusiasm' – a reference to the then prevalence of Methodism which was regarded as not the thing at all by the rural gentry and clergy, so that Wesley was denied the pulpits of country parishes. So, nothing much has changed since. Indeed, if you take the analogy of ministry anywhere as being like unblocking a spiritual well – taking out great boulders – ministry in a rural parish can be like digging a well from scratch.

In dealing with villagers who are not followers, care needs to be taken in the use of language. Alex's training incumbent Revd. Andrew Micklefield (a former Rector of Itchen Valley) warned him off against talking about ex tempore prayer and using other Christian jargon. Even such expressions as 'worship', 'growing the church', 'having a heart for' this or that and particularly 'Christian', which are in common usage in New Wine circles and have particular meanings in those circles, can result in those who are not followers being very nonplussed indeed and box the new Rector into a category in the minds of the parish, which actually reduces his influence. We may feel this is wrong and unfair, that they are wrong, but that is not the issue. The question is, 'How are we to make disciples in this place?' and using language which irritates or baffles the villagers is not helpful. The word 'evangelism' in particular can really unnerve people. An alternative might be the word 'good-newsing' because good news is the essence of what we should be about.

In summary, it is essential that a new Rector has the support of villagers who would not call themselves 'disciples' or 'followers of Christ' if the Great Commission is to be fulfilled in the community. Otherwise all the Rector's time will be taken up in keeping the show on the road – making sure the roof stays on the many church buildings and that the many services he is required to lead are conducted. The regular job needs to be carried on while disciples are being made. A favoured Rector can count on the support of many villagers to organize fundraising and other events and to put them on. They are sometimes (not always) doing it for her; to help her out. These events are born out of the relationships that the Rector develops. It is therefore important that the Rector has the vision for them and that she can inspire and encourage them.

But all of this very helpful potential support from the community can easily evaporate if the Rector is not favoured by the community. Unpopularity can take up all our time as we receive one criticism after another from all sorts of directions, by the often highly articulate professionally trained villagers around us, many of whom are retired and have the time to pursue a Rector with a vengeance, if they choose to do so. Errors in formalities, which will be generously overlooked with a favoured Rector, can be used by the legalistic as the lever to put pressure on an unpopular Rector so that eventually she gets discouraged and decides to move on.

Strangely, it matters less if the Rector lacks favour with elements of the church population, than if the non-church community don't like them. It's actually the opposite to the way that most evangelicals think. If the Churchwardens know that three quarters of the village think the Rector is brilliant, it is very difficult to put a lot of objections to what the Rector is proposing. If every time there is a large baptism service everyone goes out raving about how wonderful the Rector is; or if the schools are continually saying how brilliant the Rector is at conducting assemblies, it makes it much harder for the Rector's opponents. Some clergy worry too much about the 'old battle axes' and the power brokers in the church community. In fact, they have as much power as we give them. It's rather like the Wizard of Oz – we can invest our opponents with more power than they actually have. Behind the noise and smoke of the apparently terrifying wizard is only a little old man. If you are powerful amongst a group of ten people, who cares? It's best to look at the 100 people – who is powerful amongst them? Concentrate on being the chaplain to the community (see Chapter 5: Relationships – Be willing to be chaplain to the community) and you will find that the church will fall into line.

Good and Bad popularity Now, of course, it is the duty of the Rector to be unpopular on some occasions. There can be bad popularity and good popularity. Bad popularity is where the Rector does whatever the most influential people in the parish want him to do. Bad popularity is where the Rector seeks only to entertain, rather than to preach or teach. On controversial issues he is a pushover or wants a quiet life. He says nothing which ever challenges anyone.

We cannot be a prophetic voice into a community, without upsetting some people some of the time. We need to be able to challenge the idolatry around us and that is bound to be painful. Working out which battles to fight, which hills to die on is probably the most difficult, but also the most important task of the new Rector. Working out which non-negotiables there are in a rural context, as opposed to a city context, is critically important. But even apart from the red lines which we choose to draw, there will be things that make us unpopular from who we are: the challenging preaching, the Jesus lifestyle, speaking about Jesus in conversation. But, in addition to that, a lot of what we do should make us very popular. Everyone loves a Rector who loves them: who clearly enjoys spending time with them, who is fun, who visits them when they are sick, who encourages them when they are down. They are not interested in someone who doesn't want to invest emotionally in them. They want to do life with the Rector, not have ministry done to them. Being willing to be unpopular can be fruitful. Robin King writes: 'I remember two comments from very different people at very different times, essentially saying that they didn't like what I was doing, but they loved the effect it had. Not always doing the popular thing meant that I could do the fruitful thing, and people find fruit hard to resist'. Revd. Rupert Charkham is once said to have said 'It's no use trying to bring the good news, if you are the bad news'. Ultimately, if we are the bad news, we should probably not be trying to be a Rector in a rural community or possibly anywhere!

The most important way of ensuring good popularity is the attitude we bring to the job. We have to take relationships with our parishioners very seriously indeed (see Chapter 5: Relationships). If the community know that we love them (or at the very least like them), then we can be as prophetic as we are called to be. As John Maxwell writes, 'People don't care how much you know, until they know how much you care. You develop credibility with people when you connect with them and show that you genuinely care and want to help them'[8].

If, on the other hand, they suspect that we don't like them – then anything we say will be treated with suspicion, however valid. A rural community will be very understanding, will tolerate incompetence, inefficiency and even heresy from its clergy (although of course the Bishop and Archdeacon may have another view), particularly if we see the job as fun and have a sense of humour, but will be very unforgiving if they suspect that the Rector doesn't like them or if the Rector gets stressed about anything. Alex was told when he arrived in his parish as a curate, 'You can do anything you like but don't get stressed if things go wrong…we don't like it'. Revd. Andrew Micklefield (formerly Rector of Alex's parish) is a master at the light touch, the gentle word here and there and letting everyone know that he enjoys their company. He was very popular. If we find that, try as we might, we just don't like them, then we should try praying as hard for our own hearts to be changed so that we do, as we are praying that they will come to know Jesus. If we find that we still don't like them, then we should leave and do something else.

8. John C Maxwell, The 21 Irrefutable Laws of Leadership, p116

It is probably wise not to come to take over a rural church if we plan to coast to retirement (after hard work in an inner city – a new Rector will soon find that this is just as much hard work, surprising as this may seem) or if we have some other motivation for being there which is going to dominate our ministry, like playing golf, sailing or spending our time with our relations. It is also not wise to apply for a Rector's job if we have political or social attitudes which are going to clash with the majority of the local population. We need to be able to love the rich man in his castle, as much as the poor man at his gate – and vice versa. If we have passionate and controversial views on hunting, shooting, fishing or farming methods, then we might wisely conclude that it is best to serve God in the city or suburbs.

Having spoken at length about the importance of good popularity or community favour for a rural Rector, it is very important that this popularity cannot be an aim in itself. It is of course wonderful to be carried aloft on a tide of popularity, but ultimately the real test of a Rector's time in a parish is what continues afterwards: the church is, after all, what remains when the clergy have left. It is only in transforming the community itself, the long-term community of residents, that a Rector has done something valuable, otherwise what he has done evaporates as he packs his bags and will not survive a less favoured successor or even the vacancy in between.

The motivations of followers of Christ in the rural church In addition to villagers who would not describe themselves as followers of Christ, in each rural parish there are generally some who wonderfully would! James Campbell writes, 'Building up a core of others with a similar vision is crucial. Prayer is fundamental, both regularly with this group as well as at home, sensing where the Lord is leading; this can be lonely in the early days.'

Where you do have followers of Christ in the community when you arrive, they are such an asset and, of course, much of the time spent walking round the villages is spent praying more and more of them into the community. Whenever a house becomes vacant Ruth Guy recommends praying for people who may be open to becoming disciples to buy it and this is a prayer which she says is so often answered! As the number of followers in a community increases, the spiritual atmosphere changes and the ground for evangelism becomes easier. Quite apart from anything else, the Rector finds that he is not having to lead everything himself.

Followers of Christ (of whatever churchmanship) can have different motivations to villagers (of course it is not quite as binary as this comment would suggest). On the whole, they are not quite so dependent upon the popularity of the Rector, although this does have its limits! They see that they are in their community because God put them there and see their involvement in the church as mission. They will get on with what they feel God is calling them to do regardless of the Rector, if the Rector will let them. The biggest challenge for them is if the Rector absolutely refuses to let them act in a way that God is calling them to act. This is a very difficult situation. Many of those from HTB and New Wine churches will be praying for a Rector who at least just encourages on the side lines and doesn't get in the way; best of all someone who will encourage and pray for what they believe God is calling them to do. When buying a house in the countryside, it may be good idea to recommend to people, as a preliminary check, to meet the local Rector to see what sort of person they are before sealing the deal, or at the very least taking a thorough look at the church website as part of the due diligence on moving to a new community.

Even if we are blessed to have those who would be regular worshippers at a city or suburban church, who are keen members of home groups and would see themselves as followers of Christ, sometimes we face challenges with their priorities. Somehow with people who don't assert their faith this is less disappointing, than when they do. There is for example a real challenge with sport on Sunday mornings. We can easily have a family which doesn't think twice about prioritising little Johnnie's rugby match or cricket match on Sunday mornings even though this means that they never take part in Sunday morning worship and even though little Johnnie may be going to a school which already provides sport three afternoons a week. Even more disappointing is when one of the adults prioritises their own recreation, golf for example, over worshipping God on a Sunday. Another approach of course is to have a 'Families at Five' service on Sunday afternoons to meet the needs of those for whom children's or their own sport is such a high priority. This emphasis on sport fails to teach the children that sometimes, as followers of Christ, worshipping God needs to take priority over our recreation. Following Christ does involve sacrifice, something that every minister will know.

Another challenge comes where followers make a big point about the particular Christian virtue which they find easiest to fulfil. For example, some will emphasise the importance of giving and be quite critical of those who do not give as generously as they do. But there may be other areas in which their commitment to Christ is less than total, for example, in the way they behave to their neighbours, the priority they give to their real estate and children. Idolatry of many different kinds can stalk followers of Christ and corrupt their behaviour every bit as much as those who would not pretend to be his disciples. But it is tough for the clergy when other followers of Christ don't want to make sacrifices for the gospel. Sometimes we perceive that there is a feeling out there that 'The Rector is the professional and it's alright for him to make sacrifices, but I don't have to'. But, of course, we also could be commanding a much higher salary, a much bigger house, and much larger pension in the open market, than the nominal salary, the secondary housing and the tiny pension offered to clergy (in comparison with the villagers in Hampshire), but we have chosen not to do so. To some extent we are volunteers as well. Being part of a rural church can be quite exposing for some followers of Christ in a way that would not be the case in a city or suburban church.

Understanding the motivations and priorities of villagers and followers alike, is important if we are to be successful in steering the church towards increased engagement with Christ.

CHAPTER FIVE

Relationships

'You grow a church one relationship at a time'
Bishop Peter Hancock

As with the whole of life, running a rural church is all about relationships. Building relationships with everyone you can lays the groundwork for evangelism and new followers of Christ. It is really important that we know how to do this.

Be kind An elderly Roman Catholic priest, in response to the question from Yann 'What tips can you give me as I embark on my ministry', after a pause for thought, said 'Be kind'. There is never any excuse for being unkind in any situation, however theologically correct we might believe that we are being. We need to exercise great sensitivity in preaching and conversation, as inevitably there will be people in our congregation or community directly impacted by what we are saying, who will not necessarily accept that the Biblical witness on any issue is conclusive. Also, we are bound to make mistakes (and we should expect to make them and allow others to make them), however brilliant we are. We need to be able to apologise. If we have been kind to people, they are much more likely to forgive us than if we have not.

But that does not mean that we should shy away from speaking truth or challenging the community when the time is right. Those, like Alex, with a background as a commercial lawyer, who finds it difficult to leave a discussion with untruth still unchallenged on the table and who tends to find himself towards the truth end of the relationship/truth continuum, need to be particularly careful about this. We are never preaching or speaking to a group of people who think precisely the same as we do. So 'be kind.'

Be a friend Nicky Gumbel in his book *A Life Worth Living* points out that fellowship and mission go hand in hand in the New Testament. But we have so diminished the idea of friendship that many do not know how to develop friendships. Dale Carnegie says in his book *How To Win Friends And Influence People*[9]*:* 'You can make more friends in two months by becoming interested in other people than you can in two years by trying to get other people interested in you'. If all we do as rural clergy is to walk around being interested in people, their lives and what they want to talk about, then we are going to make friends. Friends accept invitations to do things (like attend Alpha courses) which they won't accept from strangers. If we show people that we are genuinely interested in them, then they will be interested in us and what we are

9. Op. cit. page 56

trying to do in the community. If they think that we are only talking to them for our own objectives, the whole thing backfires. One enthusiastic lay rural evangelist tells of an occasion when she made the mistake of stopping her car to speak to someone walking her dog and (without asking anything about her or her family) invited her to the next Family Service. The woman replied 'Don't you ever speak to me about this again. You are not interested in me, just getting me into your church!' Be a friend.

Be patient Rural ministry can be very active and it's difficult to be patient when so much is happening. But, nevertheless, we need to be patient and to try and take things slowly. It's about pace setting. Not being hurried when you are encountering people. James Campbell says, 'Grow relationships slowly and gain trust'. James suggests that the pace at which we should walk round our villages, is as if we are on holiday just going to get the croissants for breakfast: there is always a moment to stop to talk to someone, always time to admire a view. We may need to block out time in our diary to be able to do this – diarise space. Try to ensure that you diarise space so that you can cycle or walk around rather than drive. The video https://www.livegodspeed.org in which an American vicar, on the recommendation of theologian and author of The Message Eugene Peterson, decided to take on a parish in rural Scotland, absolutely says it all. Be patient – try to take it slowly!

Ruth Guy recommends we should 'get a friendly dog' and take it for walks every day wearing our dog collar, if we have one (so two of you with a dog collar!). This is ministry, not recreation, and thus, for a Rector, should be scheduled into our day. Everyone stops to talk to us, if we have a dog. Most importantly, allow the person we meet to set the topic of conversation.

Alex tends to say to people he doesn't recognize 'Are you a local?' before deciding whether or not to take the conversation further. It's hugely important to pray through each of these encounters and sometimes we will get a question about the church, about God, about death – this is classic 1 Peter 3:15 territory – being prepared to have an answer for the hope that we have. Alex carries on his walks a postcard-sized professionally designed calling card with details of the church's website and telephone number with him and also cards for his parish's Little Rainbows toddler group and CAMEO seniors' lunch, which can be distributed at the right moment. But we need to give people space to say no. Be very sensitive about pushing yourself on them too much.

If we assume that we have a potential relationship with everyone in the community, but they are just at different stages, we will find that every conversation brings us closer and closer until we get to the stage that we can recommend a book or encourage them to attend an Alpha. Alex has a running list of people he prays for daily for whom encounters of this kind has brought him into substantial spiritual conversations and to whom he has recommended reading material or a course. Bob Earnshaw says, 'Take time to really get to know people and get to love people, if you can. Don't get too despondent, just plough on. Whenever you get the opportunity, say something of the claims of Christ. The opportunities will come. I went in like a bull in a china shop, in hindsight it worked, but I would probably do it differently now. But God will guide you in what you do in your situation'. Be patient – take it slowly!

If we possibly can, we should learn the names of the people in the community we encounter, the names of their children, the names of their dogs and horses. If we take a note and use the names immediately, we should be able to learn them! It's difficult but pays immense dividends if we can do so.

Be willing to stay If we are being slow and growing our relationship with people so that they start to trust us, then this is going to take time. It is an enormous emotional investment in a community. It really is not a good idea to leave that community after just a few years. Stipendiary clergy are necessarily nomadic, as they don't own a property in the parish. They are almost always living in a church provided house. Alex feels that after five years in Itchen Valley he is only just beginning to get to know the community well enough and for him to be well enough known. It's difficult to set a rule because every situation is different and sometimes very fruitful ministries have been completed in a very short period of time – such as the ministry of Bob Earnshaw referred to earlier. But continuity is important and as a guide, a ten-year stint should be an aim as a minimum stay for a Rector in a rural church community (some say 8-12 years): it's a marathon not a sprint. The joy of the gospel is that it is transformational. And much of what we do in terms of transformation is evolutionary rather than revolutionary. The danger of a short-term ministry is that too much can easily be associated with the character of the individual minister and the changes that he has made can disappear very quickly. It takes time to make changes in a community where everyone else is there for ever!

Be wise Unlike in the suburban or urban church – if we have a challenging time with someone in the community – they never go away, because they live there. They are either inside the tent or outside and causing havoc! But as we get to know people and develop this hinterland of relationships with every conversation, the trivial can easily lead to the profound.

Sometimes those who don't attend church at all can become our most dangerous opponents. In one parish there was an interview in the local paper about the sad departure of a very popular young Rector. The interviewee said: 'No-one really liked her'. What was bizarre was that the individual interviewed had never, to the knowledge of the ministry team, ever set foot in the church!

Some hold resentments against the church because of something which the Rector before last did or did not do or did or did not say. This is the dark side (if you like) of so much depending upon whether the Rector is favoured or not (see Chapter 4 Starting well: The motivations of villagers). If a Rector has crossed an individual villager, it may drive that villager away from the church for years, well exceeding the term of the individual minister. We need to try to be tuned into the losses and hurts which our people suffer, however little we may see them in church. One parishioner, who is not really a regular church goer, was very hurt that the Rector did not spend time with her soon enough talking over the untimely death of her granddaughter. The hurt and anger caused by a very tragic event can get projected onto the Rector, if expectations are not fulfilled.

Sometimes you will have reported back to you, conversations which are critical about you, even the person concerned may be nice as pie to you to your face: 'Johnnie was saying to everyone yesterday that you are this or that'. Being 'wise as a serpent and as innocent as a dove' springs to mind in this context. A good policy is to treat people as if they have not said something which you know they have said, but have not said to your face. But equally we need to use this intelligence to be able to tread carefully...

Be willing to be the chaplain to the community Sometimes clergy are a bit concerned as being thought of as the 'chaplain' to the community, rather than the Rector of the parish. There is a thought that this might be demeaning in some way. No-one wants to be at the beck and call of the squire. But, actually, being a chaplain to the community as Rector is a huge privilege which means that we have a potential relationship with everyone in the villages we serve. It's astonishing that rural communities will still accept a Rector as being in this role. We are there for them, whether or not they attend our services regularly. We are not a stranger. It's a good starting point for developing a real relationship and as much worthy of a Rector's time as any work spent on those who attend our services. We have a platform into the lives of those in the community by our role which would be the envy of a city church. Alex finds that he engages with a whole series of different concentric circles of people who have differing closeness to the church: at the centre those who actually attend the services regularly (perhaps 10% of the population); then those who attend for festivals (perhaps 40% of the population) and then the rest with whom he has occasional conversations on dog walks and other encounters when out and about in the villages. The village magazine is a great way to communicate to this latter group – there is obviously the regular 'Letter from the Rectory' but Alex also has included a more secular column aimed at relationships (see the section on meeting people at the place of need in Chapter 6:

Evangelism, called 'Family File'). This gets considerable feedback from people he does not even know and gives an opportunity for follow up visits and the developing of relationships. As Dioceses increasingly want to consolidate the provision for rural ministry into market towns, it is this precious role as chaplain to the Parish – the equivalent of 'Dixon of Dock Green', the local policeman of the 1970s television series (who knows everyone and walks round the community for which he is responsible on the beat) as contrasted with 'Z Cars' (also a 1970s television series in whichever policemen are on duty come into the parish from the local town when they need to do so) – which can easily be lost as it becomes impossible for the clergy to spend time just walking round the villages and being present in the community.

The challenge, however, is the number of communities that we are dealing with. It's really a matter of dealing with expectations. As one former Archdeacon in Winchester Diocese used to say, 'When you are appointed as the Rector of a benefice of six parishes, the communities are not expecting one sixth of a Rector, but six Rectors'. Yet you are only one, hurtling from one village to another, continually disappointing everyone by the little time that you can give to each. The situation is made a lot easier if you are Rector to a merged single parish than to a benefice of several parishes as you will then be dealing with one PCC whose members have a common purpose and who are not hostile strangers to each other (we address how we might go about moving to a single parish in Chapter 12: Moving from a Multi Parish benefice to a Multi Church Parish. But even so, as being a chaplain means to be present in each of those communities, whenever there is something going on which the village is turning out for, expectations can easily be disappointed. Villagers don't understand if you are not available to attend the village fete, bonfire night, or pantomime. They tend to see things only from the perspective of their own community.

Be a pastor Pastoral ministry is so important. Alex used to think that he would be happy preaching and leading services, but as for the pastoral ministry, that would be something he would rather not do. Now he realizes that the preaching and pastoral are two sides of the same coin. We really cannot do the first, if we are not willing to do the second. We just don't know where the parish is, from a faith perspective, if we don't do the visiting. But what do we do when we do visit? There is a lot of listening and asking questions, hopefully about matters remembered from the previous occasion. With followers we can always read the Bible as well. But we can always sum up each meeting in prayer, drawing on what we have learned from the person with whom we are meeting. If the parishioner does not want us to pray with them, then Alex is inclined not to go on a subsequent visit. Although we can make a contribution to reducing loneliness, we are offering Jesus Christ, that is our job and one might think that those who actually refuse Him (and Alex has encountered some) should not take up time which could be spent on those who would.

Having a dog collar to wear in a rural community is a colossal advantage however much one may dislike clerical dress! Alex was asked at his ordination interview how he felt about cassocks and surplices – 'It's OK to say that you like them,' he was told. 'It's a sacrifice,' Alex replied. We do have to recognize that some people are going to expect us as clergy to wear robes on certain occasions. Although we can get away with not wearing them at All Age Services and anything new which we introduce, there is absolutely no point in fighting a battle over this so far as the Book of Common Prayer communion, Evensong and Matins, weddings and funerals are concerned. It's more important that the congregation hear a gospel message than what dress we are wearing when we deliver it. Yann says that at his interview he was asked by one of the patrons what was for them a key question 'Will you wear the vestments?'. His answer was 'yes' (but his thought, of course not articulated) is 'Yes, if you let me talk about Jesus I will wear anything you like'.

Walking round the community with a dog collar on means that we have conversations which we would not otherwise have. It's a bit like being a policeman on the beat. We hear what is going on in the community, it's a huge blessing. But the general principle needs to be 'deliberate' about when we wear our dog collars or wear clerical dress. Alex tends not to wear his dog collar off his patch as this could be confusing for another Rector's parishioners.

James Campbell would add a note of caution about the pastoral aspects of rural ministry, 'There are dangers. If one does any cold calling, often the only people around in the day-time, apart from the elderly, are younger mothers. In today's world, one person's word against ours can have dire consequences. I find John Mumford's '*10 Commandments for maintaining sexual purity for pastoral staff*' really useful. I recall David Prior saying that one can't avoid praying with a woman alone once – but [you] never [should] twice'.

Be Present A rural Rector needs to be seen at most village events – at the village fete, at the village pantomime and needs to be a visible presence around the place. She needs to be everywhere. Villagers will hugely appreciate seeing her on her bicycle riding round the place, ready to stop to chat. Alex regularly sits in the bar at the local pub at lunchtime once a week – ready to speak to anyone who comes in. Alex also attends the weekly café run in one of the village halls – a great opportunity to meet more people. Villagers will appreciate the Rector leading the principal weddings and funerals in the community. Failure to conduct these occasions can be interpreted as if the Rector does not care. These are key moments to get to know a wider range of villagers than would attend church.

But it presents serious difficulties if the only time that the funeral can be held is during the Rector's annual leave. Yann says that in one case he had talked over the fact with the widow that he would be absent on leave for one particular local funeral and she was very understanding, but he still thinks he was wrong not to come back from holiday to lead it. There will be many such occasions of angst as a rural rector as conflicting priorities cause challenges either for our duty to our parishioners or to our family. Our primary ministry, however, must always be to our spouse and family.

Be yourself A rural church is a goldfish bowl and everyone sees everything that is going on in our lives, whether we like it or not. But this can be a fantastic opportunity for the gospel. Whether clergy or laity, it is so important to be willing to be known and to be vulnerable. It speaks of integrity and gives a platform for all sorts of teaching. If we have had a difficult upbringing, we can be the broken child to others who are broken. Bob Earnshaw says that he was 'broken' in a number of ways when he took over the rural parish in which Tessa became a follower of Christ (as described in the Appendix). That brokenness made him a bit 'pointy', to use his words. But the Holy Spirit can use that, as we see He did with Tessa and the others who became followers in his short ministry there.

If we have experienced addiction, divorce or bereavement, this suffering can help when we take those who are suffering these terrible things through them. Alex found in his curacy that his willingness to speak about his mother's alcoholism opened up many conversations in the following weeks with parishioners. Now he finds that every aspect of his life pops up in his sermons and enables parishioners to talk to him about issues which might otherwise remain unsaid. The problem with vulnerability is that we may get hurt. But, nevertheless, we need to live in the light. Villagers will be sharing all sorts of information about themselves and it's not good if they feel that 'The Rector never reveals anything about himself'. We need to be able to be undefended. When Alex was at Theological College, the pinnacle of the practical training over the three years was a course called 'The Undefended Leader'. It's a hugely important principle. Being a rural Rector does plenty to increase a sense of personal self-esteem. It's very important that we concentrate on humility as a counter balance.

Alex was told at his ordination interview that becoming a priest was about what we are becoming as a person, rather than what we know. So, concentrating on our relationship with God is paramount, if we are to serve our parishioners to the best of our abilities. Yann says that he remembers someone at theological college saying that being a priest is all about 'inhabiting a role' but that is wrong. Being yourself is the key. Be undefended.

CHAPTER SIX

Evangelism

How do you bring people to know Jesus in the countryside? There are significant differences from a city. In the city, if a stranger comes up to you and offers to pray, then you can say 'yes' or 'no', almost certain that you will never see them again. Everyone we see in the countryside, we will see again. We might see them that evening at the pub. We may see them the following morning at the toddler group. There is history in every relationship; we are never anonymous. In the area of evangelism, nothing can be more important than the advice in Chapter 5 to 'be patient'.

A further problem is, that asking villagers who are not followers or disciples of Jesus to be evangelists (or even to pray with people on pastoral visits) is asking too much. But this may mean that the number of potential evangelists that you have in a church at the beginning is rather small. Even those who are followers may find it difficult and embarrassing to talk about Jesus with their neighbours who will still be there if they perceive that they have messed it up!

But if we look at what the Bible teaches us about

evangelism, this seems to be the policy also. In 1 Peter 3:15 we are guided to 'Always be prepared to give an answer to everyone who asks you to give the reason for the hope that you have. But do this with gentleness and respect'. The whole idea of 'Evangelism' sends many country people running screaming for the exit. There is a mixture of not thinking this is a proper thing to do (the social issue rears its head again) and being legitimately concerned about continued good relationships with neighbours. No-one in the countryside wants to have the slightest impression that their hand is being forced to believe anything. Furthermore, clergy are nomadic – just visitors really. There is a thought that 'Rectors come and go, but we are here for keeps and so why should we sacrifice our relationships with our neighbours for a Rector who may be gone in a couple of years?' A response to this might be, 'But all you have to do (according to St Peter) is to be ready to answer their questions: if they ask, then surely you can explain?' Our life as a Christian should be so obviously joyful and peaceful that others will be drawn to us and will ask questions. Work on the followership, on the discipleship, and the questions will come. But maybe there is more we can do than this. Archdeacon Robin King writes: 'My experience was…when people did go and speak (to invite people on an Alpha Course for example) their friends were open, receptive (even if they declined) and still remained friends! People always come back and say that it was easier than they expected it to be and they wished they'd done it years ago'. The other point, of course, is that we need to be willing to pray to God for people to ask us about our faith. This is a dangerous business as if we do, then they will!

In any event, we can all recognise that evangelism is a process. It's a whole series of experiences and events which come together to make the follower. Don Everts writes of five thresholds which need to be crossed before the final decision is made: from distrust to trust; from indifference to curiosity; from being closed to change to being open to change; from meandering towards seeking; and, finally, from lost to saved[10]. But the trouble with being an evangelical is that we become experts at the later stages of that process, but don't necessarily get to understand the very early stages of that process. The beginning of the process might be a little banter on a dog walk (or at the well, in Jesus' case). It might be chatting to someone in the pub. It is the delicate development of the early stages of a friendship which can lead to the asking and answering of questions which lead to faith.

Meeting people at the place of desire or at the point of need

If we were designing a soap suds advertisement for TV, we would first try and identify what people want (perhaps good-looking children in an ideal family

10. *I Once was Lost* by Don Everts and Doug Shaupp and *Breaking the Huddle* by Don Everts, Doug Shaupp and Val Gordon

life) and then show the prospective customer how she needs our soap suds to take her some of the way to get to that ideal. That's how advertising works.

Evangelism is more complicated than advertising, particularly in the rural church. Of course, the church needs to be seen to be a part of the idyll of rural life to which our parishioners are aspiring. It needs to be fun. But, also, it should appeal to the deeper desires which some of our parishioners will not even recognise that they have. CS Lewis speaks of the in-built desire or yearning in our hearts for something greater, something 'other', which cannot be satisfied by anything in the natural world. That 'argument from desire' is a well-known starting point for apologetic reasoning. In the rural church, we address this point of desire in a way which is really the essence of all evangelism, by showing our parishioners who God is and what He has done (this is the purpose of our preaching) and the part that they can have within this story, what they can do in a practical sense.

Also, wherever we are, there is a need to find meaning in a world full of suffering and the church can provide leadership in this area in showing how to address the suffering of others in our own community. This may (with the guidance of the Holy Spirit) lead them to ask questions about our motivations. Mostly, those who are not followers of Christ will not see what a wonderful Christian disciple we are in the usual run of daily life. But they are much more likely to ask questions about our faith when we spend a significant amount of time helping other people. It has been said that the health of a church can be seen in its attitude to the poor. If a church is engaging in a significant amount of social action, then those who are not Christians will notice. Nick Spencer of Theos has written a book on this subject 'Doing Good: A Future for Christianity in the 21st Century' in which he describes this approach as 'social liturgy': worship of God through helping others. His thesis is that this is the way for the church to re-engage with society and be perceived by society as doing something useful.

Alex visited the home of a young mother in the Parish who is well known for her atheism. She said, 'As you know, I don't believe in God, but I have to say I think what you in the church are doing in this parish is absolutely spot on'. It is on occasions like this that people start to ask questions which result in personal testimonies being given.

But by 'the poor' we do not mean only the materially poor (although they are at the top of the list), but the vulnerable in general. A church needs to find those in its community and beyond who are vulnerable and to care for them. This is partly because Jesus commanded us to do so – it is loving our neighbours, but also, because, in doing so, there are often opportunities to answer questions about 'the hope that we have'.

Indeed, evangelism will often start at the place of need. What we mean by this is the point where a person recognises that they don't have something which they desperately want but cannot obtain elsewhere. It may be a bit of a challenge in a commuter rural village to find this point. For many the church is providing the answer to a question which they are not asking. Most wants are fulfilled (and worries resolved) by making a bank transfer, instructing a solicitor, or seeing a doctor. But there are times when spending money or contacting professionals just does not do the trick. But how do we find out the pinch points; how do we find out the needs in a community, particularly the relatively well-off commuter rural villages in which Yann and Alex are serving?

Alex found one very reliable source of information about the needs of the community. He spoke to his hairdresser! It is something of a surprise to those who know him that he has a hairdresser at all (baldness is creeping forward with every year) but nevertheless he does. Hairdressers are the Father Confessors (or Mother Confessors) of the modern world. They are the first stop for counselling, as they are always willing to listen. Alex asked his hairdresser, 'What do you see as the biggest problems in our community?' She said, 'It's all about relationships. My clients never stop talking about problems with their marriages, with their children and their neighbours'. Subsequent conversations with the local police confirmed that the principal cause of police call outs in the area are disputes between neighbours!

This anecdotal response has turned out to be proven by statistical analysis. In 2017 Itchen Valley Parish conducted the 'Who Cares?' survey. This is a one question anonymous survey in which the clergy (and other brave parishioners) knocked at almost every door in the community to ask householders 'What hurts the most?' or 'What is the one thing in your life you find hardest to handle?'. In Itchen Valley over half of the households agreed to take part and completed the question cards which were then categorized and added to an excel spreadsheet to discover the top concerns in the community. Over 40% of the responses concerned relationships – either relationships with neighbours, or with family members. It's clear that forgiveness needs to be a top priority for teaching in the rural church. And of course, as followers of Christ, we need to model this, however hard it is.

It was identifying relationships as the big challenge in our communities that prompted Alex to run the HTB Parenting Courses for Children and Teenagers and then the HTB Marriage Course, during his curacy, as pre-evangelistic courses.

Itchen Valley ran The Parenting Children Course in February 2013, 20 people attended of whom only 10 were church goers. Parenting courses have a lot of appeal in any community. Everyone has challenges with their children and recognizes that they can learn more about parenting. The fact that the course is led on video by Nicky and Sila Lee of HTB (and was located in a church) did not seem to be an obstacle once we had started, although we did have to assure some people early on that they would not be force-fed Jesus! Once they experienced the gentle and humorous touch of the Lees, however, they were quickly reassured.

The Parish ran the Parenting Teenagers Course in October 2013 with 24 people attending. Publicity had been given not only through the church, but also through the local primary school and through the Roman Catholic network. These sorts of courses are a great way of co-operating with our Catholic neighbours.

In January 2014 Itchen Valley ran the Marriage Course. There were 17 couples for the first evening of the course, stretching our capacity to cater to the limits! Again, about half the couples did not attend church regularly and, as Alex put in his diary at the time, 'Were the younger cooler element' by which he concluded that the community consensus on these Life Courses was positive and vindicated the strategy of running the parenting courses first to get the community happy with the provenance of the course. It is so brave of any one to attend a course like this in a rural community as everyone knows that you are attending it, however much we assure everyone that the course is not only for marriages in difficulty, but to make every marriage the best it can be. Unlike the parenting courses, there is no group discussion on the Marriage Course. The Church is set out like a restaurant, with low lighting, individual low tables with candles and flowers and music playing in the background. A great atmosphere! The couples have private conversations as each topic is brought up and the music is turned up so that others cannot hear what is being said.

There was a very positive reaction in the community to the Marriage Course with articles written in the local magazine, which then eventually enabled the Parish to run Alpha in September 2014 with many people now familiar with and having confidence in the HTB way of doing things.

Meeting people at their point of need can give rise to conversations about spiritual things. It's important that the vulnerable person leads the discussion and we need to have the spiritual discernment to know when to probe more deeply. This will also help us to ascertain when someone has crossed the line into followership as well. The questions they ask, the answers they give, will be a window into their hearts which reveal where they are for the spiritually sensitive. But once this sort of conversation has begun, it becomes easy to invite them on some kind of evangelistic course or event to take them further.

Revd. Mary Cantacuzene started running 'Living with Loss' groups (LWL) about 10 years ago for people for whom the church had conducted funerals. So far, she has run three (each lasting about 2-3 years) (each time with different sets of two helpers to teach them how to run a group) until people started saying they didn't need to come anymore because they felt better! She ran them in her own home. She invited people personally, but also put an advert in the Parish Magazines as well. They met on a set night (2nd Tuesday of the month or whatever).

During this course she says she never corrected heresy (or strange folk-religion stuff about their loved-one coming back as an owl/ butterfly/ blackbird etc.) It's very common, but she just let it go past … and then when the Alpha course starts two years later it's all auto-corrected!

She doesn't look on the LWL course as evangelistic, but only a getting-to-know-you course which builds trust (albeit over a long time).

Most LWL courses are finished within about two to two and a half years as people start to say they 'Don't *need* the bereavement stuff anymore … but don't want to stop meeting!' That's when she suggests The Alpha Course and it all just keeps running but with supper and a talk or film as well as the opportunity to chat and ask any questions they like.

Whatever we discern to be the place of need in the community, it is important that we navigate the difficult line between simply doing something: running a course or providing a service, which people in the community need: social action on the one hand, and evangelism, on the other. Social action events should, if at all possible, be held in the church (if we have a reordered one which can be used for the purpose) and/or have a distinctly 'Christian' character, even though the stated aim is the action and not the evangelism. It is very easy to stray into putting on an event which does meet the needs of the community, but says nothing of Jesus. If there is any possibility that someone attending the event could leave without realizing that the event is organized and put on by the church, rather than 'people in the village', then the church should not be putting it on. Is it really mission to use precious church volunteer time and energy to set up, for example, a café in the village hall, to help reduce loneliness, when we do not make clear that it is the church running the show and that the volunteers are from the church? In a difference with the situation in a city, many villagers who are not church goers could easily be public spirited enough to organize such a thing (as has indeed happened in Itchen Valley with the wonderful 'Brew with a View' in Easton Village Hall on Wednesdays) but surely this cannot really be described as 'mission' or 'church social action', because it is not led by or staffed by church members and it is not done in Christ's name. Actual evangelistic courses such as Alpha, on the other hand, can be held anywhere (because they are self-evidently Christian) and may actually be better organized in someone's home.

If, on the other hand, a café is organised by the church and is known to be organised by the church, then there is no reason why you cannot use people who are not church goers as volunteers to help run it.

'Tea at Three' in Bentley is one such example, which works really well. The great advantage is that the non-church going volunteers get to know that the church goers are not strange in any way.

Yann has also found that he can work well with the civil Parish Council to chat about things that matter in the community. It's all very gentle. One of the products of this co-operation may be that there will be employed together a community information volunteer who would be responsible for communication across the communities of his benefice.

Evangelistic courses

Those coming from a New Wine background may see Alpha or Christianity Explored as the obvious courses to run to bring those in a rural parish to faith. However, there are those who believe that Alpha or Christianity Explored may actually be too advanced for the unchurched or de-churched communities in which we may find ourselves.

For Martin and Karen, their faith journey was 'A process and a lot of factors played a part'. In common with many of our interviewees who would self-identify as followers of Christ, they speak well of the enthusiasm of the couple who ran the family service at their local village church, Henry and Caroline Pomeroy, about their evident belief and the warmth of their welcome. The family service which they ran opened the door for families who might not otherwise have any contact with the church and who would not have taken their children to an evangelical church in the local town at that stage. However, the family service alone in the local church was not enough to take them into a real faith for themselves. 'Otherwise, when the kids grew up, that would have been the end of it', they say.

It was attending an Emmaus Course which the Pomeroys ran in their home that started the process that made a real difference. This course was advertised in the village magazine. The house group which sprang from this moved Martin and Karen on to start what they call 'Taking a grown-up interest in their faith'. But ultimately it was Alpha at an evangelical church in the local market town which enabled the penny to drop - it challenged faith assumptions, but its factual basis made a huge difference. The Pomeroys departure for Africa for several years meant that they both had to grow up as Christians and stand on their own two feet!

Of the nineteen people who would self-identify as followers of Christ who we interviewed for this book (and whose stories are told in the Appendix), and who came to faith while attending a rural church, five said that it was the way they were treated by a minister or other follower of Christ which made a critical initial difference to their journey of faith and thirteen would say that it was attending something outside church on Sunday such as the Alpha Course or a home group of some kind (with hospitality and Bible Study) which made that difference or which consolidated the impact of a particular individual. Only one interviewee would say that it was a tangible intervention of the Holy Spirit (in her case at the altar rail) that made all the difference.

Whilst the importance of what individual disciples say and do can be pivotal, it's clear that if we are serious about bringing people to become followers of Christ in the rural church, then we must also have a process by which they can become disciples. We must provide the road for the journey to take place. It must be regular and just part of the furniture of what we do. So, providing home groups and holding an evangelistic course, such as Alpha every year is really a must. The course doesn't need to be large but it does need to be regular.

Organising Alpha in the Rural Church

At the first course Alex conducted in Itchen Valley, 24 people attended of whom seven were not church goers. The course was run with speakers and not with the videos and was well received. Some thought does have to be given to whom we invite on an Alpha Course. In his previous parish, Alex used a mailing service to deliver invitations to every house in the community. It was a very expensive exercise, many of the houses never received their invitation and he received no applications for the course from any of those invitations.

Andrew Micklefield thinks (and Alex believes that he is right) that in the rural church we cannot invite someone on Alpha with integrity, unless they know us quite well. As we get to know the vast hinterland of the community in which our church is set, there are going to be those constantly coming to the top of the list who we are prompted to realise may be willing to attend such a course. Then it is probably best, when all the church goers who might want to attend have been through it, that we can turn to those who do not attend church at all.

Revd. Sally Gaze ran two courses a year in Norfolk, even though these were often very small (with 4-8 people as guests). Altogether she has run 17 or 18 courses in her benefice (starting in 2002). The challenge for her has been getting those who have been through Alpha to find the regular church appealing. She took the approach of forming cell groups and now has 60 adults and 20 young people in those groups. These groups are church – fresh expressions - for those individuals.

Not just Alpha

But we may feel that it is just not appropriate to put on an Alpha Course in our community. There is always the possibility of putting on something different.

Ruth Guy established a series of evenings called 'Food for Thought' with neutral titles such as 'Can intelligent people believe in God?', 'Is there any future for the church?'. The series of evenings was not described as evangelism and, as with Alpha, emphasized the importance of listening to and valuing the guests' points of view before trying to teach anything. The series of discussions was over four evenings and rotated for supper at different houses. There is a great appeal in the countryside to see into each other's houses and this may have accounted for the initial interest in these evenings. To follow up (instead of running Alpha) Ruth ran a course called 'Knowing God', based upon six prayers of St Benedict, but basically covering the same ground as Alpha. Ruth can point to over a dozen people who have become followers of Christ by this approach.

Revd. David Cook ran an evangelistic course in Chipping Campden called 'God in the pub'. He writes: 'I asked the PCC where might be a good venue for me to run a ten week course which I called 'Exploring Faith' - I didn't want to use the church hall. They recommended one particular pub which had a large room with a separate bar. Ideal. We had 60 people a night, mostly church members. I pitched it quite high intellectually… What do we mean by God? Who was Jesus? Can we trust the New Testament? I followed this course in the new year by another in a different pub. I called this one 'Discovering Faith'. It lasted four weeks and was evangelistic and it was based on John's Gospel….. We had about 30 or so attending'. One of those whose testimonies are given in the Appendix, Tim Binder, came to Christ at this event.

Tim Binder writes 'My next door neighbour Mike

would invite me for a meal on Tuesday evenings while my wife was away. One such evening, Mike invited me to one of David Cook's 'God in the pub' talks in the Seymour Arms in Chipping Campden. David was talking that night on John 4 (now my favourite chapter in the whole Bible!). I had never listened to such a real and living exposition of any part of the Bible and I was so fortunate to hear David do such a good job of it that evening. The more he spoke the more relevance that chapter had on my life; it really spoke to my condition. At the end of his talk David said a short prayer of commitment saying that if anything we had heard that night resonated with us then just say 'Amen' to the prayer. I did and felt that metaphorical rucksack shift and slip. On the way back home, I said to Mike: 'I think I just met God in the pub.'

David Cook continues: 'A year or so later I ran an Alpha course in the original pub, followed by different series...some better than others. Basically, I used three different pubs in Chipping Campden, but also ran an evangelistic course in a pub in Ebrington, a small village of which I was also the vicar. At least two people came to faith as a result of this course. Back in Chipping Campden over the years I got outside speakers to cover such topics as Science and Faith, Other Religions, the Problem of Suffering, the Financial crash of 2008, etc. I had people give testimonies etc. Some series were better attended than others. Some were fruitful in putting the church on the map and at the very least making people think! I'm not sure who might have found a faith as a result though! And, on the whole, we didn't draw many people from outside the church. Those who came were either church members or people who had a link somehow with the church. For what it's worth I also got Jonathan Aitken to come and speak in Chipping Campden. For this I hired the large school hall, and it was packed!'.

Bruce Newson says in his parish, that it was a simple Lent Course which made the difference for him and his wife: 'It was not the opportunity to study the Bible that caught our attention but the location of the course on each of the evenings. As you might expect, in this wealthy part of Hampshire, most of the villages have some very fine historic houses and they were a fascination to those of us who had moved into the countryside from a densely populated coastal town. And so fascinated were we that we could not pass up the opportunity to see the inside of these country homes with their large estates. So it was for that reason we enlisted in the Lent course of 1986, to see how 'the other half lived'. That was the start of a journey which has led him and his wife to faith and for him to become a Licensed Lay Minister.

Drip drip drip and apologetics

But it is not just in what may be called 'process evangelism' or 'evangelism by course' in which people can become followers of Jesus Christ in rural communities. The rural church has given Yann an opportunity to see what he describes as 'another slice of Spirituality'. Bringing people to discipleship in the rural community can also be achieved in a different way to the approach taken in the city. Yann says that his view of making disciples has become more rounded and informed by his time in the rural church.

One churchwarden in Yann's churches is on a particularly interesting journey. He went on his first Alpha course a year or so ago and loved it. But it was not Alpha which caused the transition, but rather the drip, drip, drip of constant Bible preaching over a long period. Yann says that apologetics has been the key for this individual and many others of his congregation. Realising that there is good evidence to take the Bible seriously is quite a surprise to a lot of people in the rural church, given the constant barrage in the media undermining the authenticity of the Bible and the work of Richard Dawkins and other militant atheists. Yann has run a course on liturgy. It's a great opportunity to say to his people 'Did you know?' and, generally, of course they did not!

What is interesting for Yann is to watch this parishioner with his increasingly more dynamic faith and how he is now expressing it. He is just as frustrated about the lack of flexibility amongst his brethren, as Yann is. However, one Sunday he read from the King James Version of the Bible which Yann says, 'He knows winds me up' but the churchwarden said 'But this passage is so well known and the language flows so beautifully, so I am going to read it from here'. Yann's observation is that what is beautiful is that God working in him is allowing him to make his own decisions about things in ways which reflects the power of the Holy Spirit in his life. He is not necessarily coming to the same conclusions that Yann would come to about how we should do something, but yet God is in there. It's driven by faith and the Kingdom rather than culture and habit now. Why not celebrate the old King James Version and its beautiful language?

He has become a good critical friend to have who challenges Yann on the charismatic and evangelical cultural assumptions that Yann has brought to the parish. But he does this from a position of genuine faith enquiry and a seeking heart rather than just being there for the ride. He can see the evidence of testimonies and things that have happened in prayer meetings in Bentley and weighs these and asks questions. It is very easy from an evangelical perspective to see someone who does not speak the same language as someone who has not 'crossed the line' into followership. But, in fact, that is to make the same error of not looking beneath the surface, not looking under the bonnet, as it were, to see whether a genuine transformation has occurred, which it may have done, but the transformation just doesn't look identical to the transformation which occurred in our own lives. God is a god of limitless variety, in the spiritual as well as the physical realms. This is not about us all getting to the same churchmanship.

Making drizzle cake and disciples

In the city there can be a sense that because people have done Alpha and joined a house-group and have been evangelistically processed, then they have necessarily got somewhere spiritually. But this is not the only way. When Jesus begins something in the life of one of his children even the quite ordinary things become spiritually significant, even making lemon drizzle cake! Yann tells the story of how he told a lady in his parish: 'You make lemon drizzle cake so well and, if you can do it for the Kingdom, it will take on a life of its own'. And it did. Now when there is a catering opportunity, the lady concerned knows that it is spiritually significant. She does five times the amount of catering that she used to do, and she loves it and is buoyed up by it!

We need to get the church away from the idea that it is only the vicar who does spiritual things in the church. For some this is a way of pushing away the responsibilities of becoming a disciple of Jesus. For example, someone in the church may say 'I'm not going to pray for anyone, that's for vicars to do'. But for others it's a block to their own spiritual journey. Hospitality is a hugely significant gift. The lady concerned sees that God has given her the talent for cake making and cares about her even though she was not a priest or some kind of professional religious person. She now knows that she matters. Think of all those meals that Jesus ate! We need Marthas as well as Marys! The mature disciple knows when to be a Mary and when to be a Martha. Both are needed. Part of the skill of the Rector is to identify those people who have particular skills which can be used for the Kingdom, rendering them spiritually significant. This can be the start (as it has been for the lady concerned) of a journey of discipleship or even a journey of vocation. And, of course, it is not just drizzle cake makers on this journey. Yann speaks of someone in his church who rarely speaks but gives his time providing the audio-visual service for the church. This is 'one of the most releasing things we have in our church' Yann says. 'He does it brilliantly and gives hours and hours and hours to this work. Without him we would not be able to operate'.

But the drizzle cake makers and the AV experts and all those journeying through spiritually significant work need opportunities to be encouraged and developed, to meet with others and to pray together. Although there is a certain amount of this that we can do on a Sunday, mostly this has to be done during the middle of the week either by mid-week services or home groups.

Home Groups

Whether people are attending home groups or not is a good test of whether they are becoming followers of

Christ. Early in Revd. James Campbell's time in (what is now) Bentley, Froyle and Binsted benefice, in 1995, Christopher and Kathy Ogilvie Thompson returned to their family home in the parish. There were no home groups running at this time. Now there are almost 100 parishioners in home groups in the benefice. It is an astonishing result and a real indication of the spiritual health of the benefice. Of course, a group of retired people meeting during the day may not indicate anything about their commitment to Christ (as they could be just looking for entertainment and company) but certainly if someone who works is giving up a precious evening, this is a very good indication of a commitment to being a disciple. There are twelve home groups altogether in Bentley, Froyle and Binsted comprising five groups meeting during the day and seven groups meeting during the evening.

But how did this get started? In the mid 1990s James Campbell started running once a term mid-week topical talks with a meal which were open to anyone in the community at one of the larger homes in the benefice. All the evenings had some kind of Christian input. There was often a well-known speaker. When Jonathan Aitken came to speak, for example, about 80 people attended, but often the audience was around 40. But getting speakers was really hard work.

These topical talks enabled James, Mary Campbell, Christopher and Kathy to achieve credibility in the community and get people into the habit of coming out to events organised by the church. People got to know them better. They started to realise that although they were followers of Christ, they 'didn't have two heads'.

Then the team started Alpha courses in parallel with the social evenings, using the audio tapes which were then available (this was back in the early days of Alpha). James started with inviting the existing church congregation because those were the ones with whom he was in contact most. But the effect was that by doing this, James gained confidence that most of the congregation had heard the whole gospel, providing a solid foundation for his preaching on Sundays. Then there were more Alphas (perhaps once a year) encouraging the congregation to get involved in helping, if they had been part of the earlier course. Christopher and Kathy say that, in their experience, it seems to take on average two and a half Alphas for people to get it and become followers of Christ!

At some stage one house group started during these early days. It was a group of about 10 or 12 die-hards. As now, the question was asked towards the end of Alpha, 'Would you like to continue meeting?'

Also, during this time, during Lent, because people were anxious about the open-ended commitment that a home group might involve, James ran a book club with lunch and discussed one chapter of the book a week. There would be smaller day time Alpha courses particularly for women, these groups would tend to continue meeting after Alpha had been completed.

In about 2004, the team started running the Marriage Course. Again, this did much for the credibility of the team and for the courses run by HTB. People realised that they were not threatening and running this course led to openings to invite people on Alpha.

One year, when proposing to do an Alpha for men and women, only men showed an interest in attending. Accordingly, the team decided to start in the pub with a pint and then go on to someone's house for the course. Perhaps 12/13 men attended that Alpha. After that only one of the men had become followers of Christ. Most of them were still very cynical but, surprisingly perhaps, wanted to carry on meeting – to argue! So, for two and a half years they continued to meet regularly for a meal and a glass of wine. It was the friendship and fellowship, doing the journey together, which they wanted. Half of the men had spouses who were followers of Christ, who were, of course, praying them into the Kingdom. Then there was a breakthrough. One of the men took a trip to South Africa and on a whim attended a conference led by the farmer evangelist Angus Buchan, the author of Faith Like Potatoes. He came back so touched and changed by this experience, 'It's all true', that he enthused the rest of the group, who all moved forward to followership at that point. Then the men's group was blessed by some established followers joining who came from outside and the group had got too large and needed to be split – three ways!

One of the women in the benefice felt God calling her to start a group for young mothers and also for women whose husbands were not interested in Christianity and so did not want to come out to an evening group or church on Sunday mornings. This in time also grew into three groups. Then there was another group for women whose circumstances had changed, because they had now gone back to work and, having met during the week, now wanted to meet in the evenings. Then there were subsequent home groups of men and women which arose from mixed Alpha courses. More recently, another group started for a particular person who needed support, which then grew into something more.

Evening home groups in Bentley, Froyle and Binsted tend to start at 7.30pm with a meal with wine or at least refreshments. Sometimes, just soup and bread is served but generally the men need something more substantial. Either way, eating together is very important and makes a difference. This is a time to talk and slow down and eat after getting off the train and a busy day at work. The day time groups tend to have coffee and cakes. Most of the groups last about 2 hours long and end with a time of prayer. This is the time when the pastoral care side of things is being fostered. Everyone takes a shot at leading the group.

One challenge is to keep all the groups synced with the teaching in church, particularly where there is a sermon series going on. When there is a sermon series going on in church, the groups are all encouraged by the team to follow the accompanying study guides, but there are other times of year when they can follow whichever books they prefer.

But coordinating this requires a lot of forward planning, which may not always be possible. Indeed, a whole term's notice may be needed to turn all these home groups so that they are all pointing in the same direction!

But organising all your groups to point in the same direction may seem like a problem which is a long way off for many rural parishes who only have one or two home groups, if any: a good problem to have!

CHAPTER SEVEN

The Holy Spirit in a rural context

Strange manifestations How does the Holy Spirit guide and impact the rural church? Revd. Sally Gaze says that 'Rural church members will sometimes be very wary of talk of the Holy Spirit…this happens when they associate talk of the Spirit with waving hands in the air, bizarre manifestations and guitar-led hard to sing choruses. These can be embarrassing in a small congregation'[11]. But when we see the Holy Spirit in action, He has a profound impact on a rural community.

The Holy Spirit at work in the community There is no greater friend to the rural Rector than the Holy Spirit. Every time we step out of the door, we need to be asking the Holy Spirit to show us where He is working in the community; to give us an opportunity to speak of Him to someone. We will be asking Him to tell us what to say to an individual. Whether to approach them or not.

During his curacy, Alex found himself taking the dog for a walk around the village and muttering to

11. Op. cit. page 7

himself about someone in the church and he felt God say to him 'By this people will know that you are my disciple – that you love one another…!' He felt a bit corrected and said to the Lord 'Ok, if you are working in this place, then show me, by arranging things so that I have shared my testimony by the time I get home from this walk'! So, he turned round the corner, and there was a group of cyclists hanging around the entrance to a house. They then left on their ride, leaving the wife of one of them, who is lovely, but not perhaps a regular church goer, wanting to chat. They spoke together about churches which are growing and churches which are shrinking, and she said to him; 'I have heard it explained like this: becoming a Christian is like seeing a complicated mathematical equation on a chalkboard. You look at it and look at it and just can't understand it. It makes no sense at all…then someone comes and explains how it works, then suddenly you understand - the penny drops...' Then she said 'So how was it for you, how did you become a Christian..?' So, he shared his testimony. It is by these wonderful glimpses that we in the rural church see that God is working in our parishes.

More recently, Alex found himself walking past a woman in her forties who looked so sad that he introduced himself to her. She explained the very tragic turn that her life had taken and soon he found himself praying for her on the path, in the open. A further encounter, which also led to prayer, occurred when asking someone he encountered on a walk a question which was misunderstood to be a question about her husband, whereupon she burst into tears to reveal an unfolding tragedy revealed to no-one before. Another random encounter of this kind has indirectly led to Alex being interviewed for a radio podcast on what it means to be a disciple of Christ.

Revd. David Watson's mantra, as he walked round St Cuthbert's Church York in 1965 as the newly appointed curate in charge, with the representative of the Church Redundancy Commission with a view to closing it down within 12 months was 'If anyone comes to this church and preaches the simple gospel of Christ, believes in the power of prayer and trusts in the Holy Spirit, this building will be full in no time'[12]. By 1971 the little church was saturated with a regular church population of over 200 and a move needed to be made. The move to St Michael Le Belfrey.

Sensitivity to the Spirit is perhaps the most important requirement of the Rector. As Robert Murray McCheyne wrote, 'The greatest need of our parishioners is our own personal holiness'.

Healing There is nothing more striking for non-believers than the healing ministry of the Holy Spirit, but we may need to be a little brave to introduce this ministry to them.

In July 2014 during a vacancy in his Parish, Alex heard that one young mother, Sonia, (who had only one operating kidney which was in decline) needed to

12. *You are my God* David Watson page 74

go on dialysis: a very unpleasant situation for a young woman in her thirties with two young children. It occurred to Alex that the parish as a whole should be invited to pray for her. An email invitation was sent out to as many people as possible setting up a day of prayer for her and asking for volunteers to sign up to pray for an hour (or in an hour) for her over a 24-hour period. Sample prayers were offered and it was arranged for parishioners to have the churches open longer on the day of prayer, if they felt that they needed to go there to do their stint. When Andrew Micklefield (who was still on the email distribution list as the former Rector) received the email, he told Alex later he had thought 'Ooh, I wonder how that is going to go down in Itchen Valley?'. But despite the reservations about taking this action, the 24 hours were soon filled, sometimes by people Alex had never seen in church before.

But, of course, it was disappointing when God did not provide an immediate solution to this problem. And, as Alex left for HTB Focus in August, he was cross and gloomy. It had seemed so amazing that so many people in the Parish had been willing to sign up to pray for her, an activity which was way outside their comfort zone, particularly since many of them were not regular church goers. Of course, these are difficult prayers to make. Finding the blessing of a transplant kidney only arises from another's tragedy. So, the prayer was not for a kidney to become available (i.e. for someone to die) but from among tragic circumstances that would occur for there to be a kidney available for Sonia. However, Alex was cross all the way to Kent, where Focus was being held that year, from what he felt was a lack of response from God to the passionate prayers of the community. But on the journey, he felt God saying to him 'So, it's ok if its Marina's kidney is it?' Marina is Alex's youngest daughter. So, he replied 'No, of course not'. God seemed to say, 'Think about what you are asking me!' Suitably admonished, Alex noted that every talk and featured book that year at Focus seemed to be about humility! It was quite a lesson.

Strangely, despite the predictions of the doctors, Sonia did not feel the need to start dialysis until the beginning of September. This sent Alex into a further spin of discouragement. He wrote in his prayer diary at the time 'I feel as if all my efforts for the gospel in the Valley are coming to nothing. I wonder whether you anointed me to carry out this task at all…what was the point of the prayer day for Sonia, if it is not answered in any way, Lord!'.

But on Sunday morning 14th September, there were a series of telephone calls from Mike, Sonia's husband. The hospital had found a kidney for Sonia and she was going to have the operation while we were all in church worshipping at a family communion. 'Could we all pray for her?' he asked. And immediately after the successful operation, Mike's constant refrain was 'Prayer really works!'. Her surgeon described the operation as the ‘perfect kidney at the perfect time’ with a very low likelihood of failure. Sonia said that all the other patients she saw at the hospital had been waiting for years on dialysis for a kidney. She only had to wait for 11 days! At the time of writing five years later, Sonia continues to flourish with her new kidney and continues to be grateful to God for it.

It was an astonishing result of God’s great generosity in response to our prayers. It had been definitely worth taking the risk of asking the parish to sign up to a 24-hours of prayer. The first Alpha course in the Parish for some time started a few days later and this was naturally an important topic of conversation.

Sometimes though the wonderful prayed for results do not happen, but perseverance provides its rewards. In Yann’s parish a gardener contracted a mysterious illness the origin of which was never ascertained. His body was shutting down and soon went into a coma. Yann went up to the hospital and prayed for healing and anointed him. A prayer meeting was called together, and all sorts of people turned up. All the regulars you would expect and others. But he died.

A couple of months later, the gardener’s father had meningitis and was of course also taken to the hospital and went into a coma. Yann went again said the same prayer and did the same anointing. He called together another prayer meeting. The same people came. Just as Yann was about to leave the consultant called his relations and said, ‘You need to get ready for the worst’.

But he recovered. The group who had been praying for him were amazed.

Another young man (aged 34) had cystic fibrosis. His situation deteriorated badly one Summer. He just survived the Summer, relying on oxygen bottles etc. As December came round, things got so bad that Yann saw that the parents had actually lost hope. The consultant had advised that the son would only live for a few days at best. Yann held the prayer meeting. Two days later he was getting a transplant, despite his infection levels being sky high.

We may not be able to do the five step John Wimber model of conducting healing in the rural church, but we can get the community to pray! Getting a community to pray for the sick has an impact, even if there is no healing this side of Paradise. There is an effect in the heart of the person who is being prayed for and an effect in the heart of the people who are doing the praying, regardless of whether there is a cure or a solution to the illness. A rural Rector can call the community to prayer; not every week, perhaps. But in Yann's parish there were these three specific events when the community came from all over the place to join together in prayer for the sick. It was very powerful. The intriguing thing is what happens when you bring God into something which occurs naturally – people will turn up to help and the Holy Spirit can do the rest.

Of course, healing is not the only ministry of the

Holy Spirit. Is there a place for praying in tongues in the rural church? Perhaps this is really where the principle element of conflict arises around the Alpha course in rural church situations and so some caution needs to be exercised in talking to church goers about this subject. However, Yann says that he does pray in tongues all the time: at the communion rail; when lost for words in intercessory prayer – on many occasions. But most of the time he will not be praying in tongues audibly. The place to engage with this sort of charismatic worship is probably on Alpha or in a home group rather than in the regular services of the church.

Yann also conducts prayer ministry in the church. It's conducted a little bit out of the way in a prayer corner, but people are quite comfortable with it. What's fun about this is the way that one of the churches has organised a prayer area - its decorated like someone's snug. Prayer ministry is conducted at the end of every service. People don't have an issue about it.

Alex has started a group to pray for 30 minutes at lunch time once a week for the parish. The prayer is conducted ex tempore and is then followed by a period of listening to God. The words and pictures which this group has spoken out in this brief moment of charismatic prayer have been as St Paul suggests they would be in 1 Corinthians, edifying for both him and the parishioners involved. In fact, many of these words and pictures have pointed towards solutions for apparently intractable problems within the parish. Whilst when Alex tends to pray in silence asking for some kind of picture, he tends only to receive an impression of a puddle of water, others in this group have had the most spectacular and wonderful images. Seeing these different talents manifested in a group he had called together has really demonstrated for him the variety of talents which are given to the 'Body of Christ'.

CHAPTER EIGHT

Introducing lively services into a rural parish

A good question to ask ourselves if we are running a local church is 'Are we mirroring the census?' In other words, does our church population have the same proportion of young and old, as the civil population? If the church is for everyone, then it should. However, new generations (particularly the so called 'missing generations' of teenagers, students and young adults and, even, thirty and forty year olds) do not necessarily engage with the church in the way that their parents and grandparents are used to and are bored with formal liturgy. It's no good saying to them 'Just get them used to our way of doing church' – they would simply prefer to stay away.

So, we need to find new ways of engaging with these generations. We need church services which are fun, but not superficial; which are about worshipping God, but not necessarily in the way that He has been always worshipped in the past. We need to experiment and be willing to try new things.

Andrew Micklefield used to say, 'We try things, but we don't worry if they don't succeed – we just try something else'. It's a good policy for the rural church, where we will be constantly surprised by the effectiveness of some approaches which we felt were doomed to be rejected by the community and astonished by the failure of others which we felt bound to succeed.

Revd. Chris Dudgeon writes: 'We launched a new Informal Service at All Saints Church in Odiham, a rural parish in Hampshire, in mid-2014. From the outset this has been a regular weekly service at 11.15am every Sunday morning, with the objective of offering a more informal style of worship than our existing 9.45am Parish Communion and the 8am BCP Communion weekly services.

'We started out with a small group of about 10 in this new congregation and have now steadily grown to a weekly congregation of about 50-60, including an average of 10 children. 'Most growth is currently occurring amongst families with children under seven, although with a newly appointed Youth Pastor in our benefice, the upper age of our children is steadily increasing. Growth has been mainly through additional people coming to church, with almost no transfer from other services at All Saints, or from other churches.

'Our informal services follow a regular pattern of six key components, which include welcome and introduction with a relaxed 'meet and greet' time, a time of extended sung worship and prayers, an ‘encouragement spot’ which is ‘open mike’ time to share testimonies and answers to prayer and encouraging videos, a talk preceded by a Bible reading, and finally a close and blessing, followed by an invitation for prayer ministry. The service aims to offer something for all ages rather than being a ‘family service’, and so the children stay in for half the service and then mostly all go out to enjoy separate children’s church activities, whilst the adults enjoy a further time of worship and teaching, and the children then rejoin towards the end of the service.

‘We did not have worship leaders available at the start of this new service, but instead discovered and have been greatly blessed by music provided by iSing Worship, which we continue to use today. iSW have re-recorded 160 songs, ranging from the latest worship songs to traditional hymns, using a professional band, and providing synced lyrics and backgrounds which we find work seamlessly using the screen and projector which we have installed in the church. The songs can be set up in advance on an iPad, PC or Mac, and the operator can follow this pre-set pattern or have the flexibility of a worship leader to repeat or remove choruses and verses as they feel led during the worship. It has been a wonderful resource and has provided us with a superb quality of music and worship leading from the outset, and people have even asked us where the band were standing as they couldn’t see them!

‘There are four key components that we feel

have underpinned growth in this new informal congregation. The first is a focus on prayer, and we are strengthening our focus on this as a key priority. The second is a focus on welcoming newcomers and helping them to become quickly involved in serving – joining what we call the Engine Room, which is essentially joining a serving team. We also have regular socials, where we aim to get the whole congregation together, normally for lunch quarterly after the Sunday service. The third is a focus on children and youth, where we have invested in children's church, and as this is an informal service, we aim to make children feel excited and involved, and their parents relaxed about noise and moving around! Finally, we are encouraging all in this new congregation to deepen their faith and to grow as disciples, and we have launched new programmes to support this such as Alpha, Bible in One Year, and new home groups, and we are finding that this is also supporting continuing growth.'

Itchen Valley Parish has had a lively All Age Worship service once a month for some years. It involves contemporary worship led by a band with minimal liturgy and a talk aimed at 8-year olds. The expressed intention is to get the teenagers involved in the band (great audience experience for anyone learning an instrument and so popular with parents) and for the younger children to see the teenagers still involved in church creates a healthy cycle. This is a well-attended service and draws in a lot of the younger parents who we would not normally expect to see at our traditional services.

During her time in the parish, Revd Amanda Denniss started a service in Itchen Valley Parish called 'Valley Worship'. This was expressly aimed at the younger parents. Again, the Band was involved but with no teenagers this time. The Sunday school, the Ark, and the youth group UTX (Under the Cross) operate during this service. So, the talk is aimed at the adults. It is hoped to attract more young parents by offering bacon butties or mini pastries before the service and football on a nearby sports field afterwards to attract the fathers and sons (and of course also the mothers and daughters). One element is a 'Every Day Lives' slot when someone from the congregation is interviewed to see what they will be doing at the same time on Monday and what being a Christian means to them in their work place/life.

Yann started something called 'Live at Five' which was lay led. It replaced the busiest morning service and is run every other week. Sandwiches and cake are served. Tea for children is given at 4.30pm so that parents don't have to feed the children when they go home. Yann says 'The cake is unleashed at 4.45pm and at 5pm the service starts. Children are running around and have toys and activities at the back of church. It's a bit of a free for all. There is a block of contemporary worship. Then they usually have a fun thing – rapid fire questions – 'East Enders or Coronation Street/

Fried or boiled' etc – it's a very clever way of getting to know people. Then 'Tea duelling'. If the biscuit drops in the tea you are disqualified. Everyone is involved – the whole family. Then there is a reading and a short talk about 10 minutes which we try and supplement with a video if possible. We do a tiny bit of liturgy in the form of a contemporary creed or a canticle; a few intercessions hopefully creative and finish at six pm on the dot!' The idea of Live at Five was principally to attract touch line Dads, but this may not have been achieved. What was very surprising was that when he moved this service from the local school and the morning, to the afternoon and to the church, Yann found that the attendance went up. The congregation now averages about 60 plus at Live at Five.

Even in the most traditional of environments we can introduce new practices to more traditional services which open up a totally new window on the worshippers' spirituality. Yann asked the worshippers of Froyle to bring the service card up to the altar rail when receiving communion if they wanted prayer for something. This was to be the sign for the Eucharistic Assistant that they should give the wine, but also pray for the communicant. The churchwarden was very sceptical as to whether anyone would do so. But a quarter of the congregation came forward with their cards!

There is nothing wrong with middle of the road Anglican liturgical services, however dull we might think they are. The problem is when God is excluded. There is nothing wrong with a bit of dull liturgy because bringing the Holy Spirit into things transforms even this! Even with all the modern prejudices that we might have against the Book of Common Prayer Communion Service, if we really sit there and allow God to speak to us, it is rich and its meaty. Alex was delighted and astonished when returning to the BCP for the first time after becoming a follower of Christ at the end of the 1990s. It is so challenging – and the words 'If you are in love and charity with your neighbours' always seem a good check on stepping forward for communion. It's good stuff. If you are a new vicar in a parish which has not had the gospel, you are bringing in the Kingdom to everything.

But are we pouring new wine into old wine skins? Sally Gaze managed to keep the show on the road in her rural churches in Norfolk maintaining the old services, but created something new, which ran alongside. Yann says that his understanding on coming into his job in Bentley was that you gently, lovingly manage the death of the old, while giving birth to something new. But what he is discovering is that God is bigger than that and there is room for the new wine, in the old. But perhaps the new wine/old wineskin paradigm is about our hearts, rather than about the church. It's about personal transformation at the end of the day. God can do anything, even within the existing structures. James Campbell says, 'Now I am less convinced that forms of service are key: changed hearts are.'

Indeed, this is a general principle which can be applied to a lot which we experience in the rural church. When Yann left Wycliffe, he could not possibly have imagined conducting a pet service. However, now he sees this as an evangelistic opportunity to reach people who would not normally attend any sort of service. If you bring God into the traditional, the naturally occurring, you change its nature. If God is the creator of all things, then He can be worshipped through anything which is created, or which is naturally occurring. The same service can be just entertainment for country people, which is not what the Rector is there to do; but can also be an evangelistic opportunity, depending upon whether we invest it with God. 'I am now excited about pet services' Yann says. But how does he do this? He is not sanctifying the pet, but giving thanks for it. He talks about God the Creator and gives thanks for the dog or cat and prays that the pet will remind the parishioner of God. Alex has found himself blessing a pack of beagles (largely a prayer of thanks for the wonderful countryside and for safety as the beaglers go about their activity). Yann says it's a bit like St Augustine's experience in coming to England in the sixth century. He invested local pagan practice with the Christian God. Our culture has been formed as a result.

CHAPTER NINE

Occasional offices, annual events, graveyards and how to use them for Christ

Occasional Offices are great opportunities to get to know local families really well and thus possible steps on the path of evangelism. It is so important for the Rector to conduct these events himself and not leave them to outsiders or previous clergy. Failing to do so can easily be misconstrued as not caring. Yann still feels bad that he did not conduct the funeral of a very significant person in the church who died and whose funeral needed to be conducted during his leave. He chose not to do so after a lot of discussion with the bereaved spouse. Managing boundaries is one of the greatest challenges for the rural Rector. But perhaps without managing the boundaries for his family, the Rector will end up failing to be able to do his job at all.

Yann has spoken to over 20,000 people at weddings. The evangelistic opportunity of weddings should not be overlooked. Weddings are good for the parish as they result in a steady stream of young couples coming into and ultimately joining the church. But they are resource heavy. Weddings are helpful for the congregations because they help them to share hospitality and give others an impression of the character of the church in the welcome that they receive. 'People always talk about the welcome'. It shows how a small seemingly insignificant parish can have an influence beyond its boundaries. Yann says that one couple has actually moved into Binsted because they were married there. This would not have happened if they had held their wedding ceremony at their reception venue.

In the funeral or wedding service, it is important to 'get the balance right' in the Address. As Revd. Mike Lloyd (now principal of Wycliffe) says 'Don't get at people at these services'. It is perfectly possible to preach the gospel, for the talk to have a substantial gospel message, but also to be light hearted, humorous (perhaps not so much at a funeral, although there is often a desire amongst the bereaved for a light touch in the leadership of a funeral) and personal to the family itself. It is perfectly possible to delight the family and believe that you have honoured God and preached the gospel in the process, even in the very short period available for a sermon at a cremation. A good book to read about how to conduct funerals is 'Accompany them with Singing' by Thomas G Long. James Campbell always insists on a gospel slot at funerals, he writes, 'At some funerals the family are not keen and do even remove the Address from the Order of Service! My technique is to separate the person, if I am speaking about them, from the Gospel, unless they have a real faith.'

James Campbell writes, 'Do get the names correct! In one service, the deceased's son came up during the first hymn with a note, 'My father was called [say] 'Jim' – I'd forgotten to clarify what Frederick James Smith was [usually called]'.

If we possibly can, we need to be flexible to what the family wants in funerals and weddings. There is a bare minimum to a Church of England occasional office, but there is no point in upsetting people by saying 'no' unless we absolutely know that what they are asking is not possible. Equally, we do need to be aware of what the Churchwardens feel about these services as well. A carefully negotiated funeral (or memorial stone) with distressed relations can come unstuck if the Rector does not know where the Churchwardens boundaries of good taste lie.

Baptism is so important. It is that moment when new parents often first appreciate their own mortality. On the theme of flexibility, views on what approach to take to baptisms vary. It's been a bit of a source of discussion between the writers of this book! Canon law says 'wherever possible' a baptism should be conducted in the main service of the parish on that day. Some take the view that a distinction should be drawn between those who are resident in the parish and those who are not. Many families will see their parents/grandparents/ aunts/cousins house in the countryside as their 'family home' to which they return for holidays and on special occasions. But it is unlikely that they will ever become part of the church congregation, because they actually live in London or elsewhere miles from the parish. Insisting upon holding their child's baptism in the main service can be disruptive to what we are trying to do with the congregation who live in the parish, and upsetting to the family, creating a negative impression of the church. Bob Earnshaw thinks that the strict baptism policy that he adopted in the 1980s in the rural church, which included insisting that families attended the church on a number of occasions before the baptism in the main service itself was, in retrospect, a mistake. This was the catalyst for his early departure from that particular benefice. So that view says try and determine whether there is a real possibility that this family will become regular church goers in our church before deciding whether holding the baptism in the main service is an appropriate way to introduce the family to the local church. James Campbell writes, 'Baptisms have many pitfalls, especially if one operates an open policy as I have. [Once I was asked to see a parishioner's] daughter and future son-in-law about getting married. The latter was a non-practising Muslim. I should have said 'No' immediately rather than having a lengthy, inconclusive meeting. We ended up with an unhappy family and one less [parishioner].'

Others take a different approach and question whether allowing private baptisms under any circumstances is dishonouring to God. So that view says that all baptism should be conducted during the morning worship service. In any event, it makes no sense to conduct a baptism during communion because it makes the service long and is not very hospitable to the guests.

How do we decide which way to go on this issue? The challenge with all questions of this kind is that there is a point in our ministry that we have to decide: is it most honouring to God to be right theologically or to allow yourself to be misunderstood and misappropriated?

Baptism preparation is very important since many young couples have absolutely no idea that more is involved than a simple naming ceremony. The key question is usually around the godparents – that they are required to be baptised themselves (and ideally confirmed). Alex recently had one couple who asked if someone who was Jewish (by religion) could be a godfather. The answer was obviously 'no' but was met with incredulity! But new parents are often at a stage when they are reflecting on life and its purpose when faced with the birth of their first child. We can discuss metanoia with the couple – change of mind – this is a time for repentance and dealing with eternal destiny for the child but also for the parents. It is clearly an evangelistic opportunity to be handled, as always, with sensitivity.

The number of adult baptisms and confirmations is a bit of a guide on whether people are becoming followers or not. Alex encountered one middle aged man that he knows quite well (and who he has always known to be an agnostic) who recently was confirmed in a neighbouring benefice and asked him about his journey of faith. 'Nothing much has changed' he replied, 'It just seemed the right time to get this done'. So, we cannot be sure that conducting these church offices necessarily give us a window into whether someone has come to faith or not. Perhaps this is why the Baptists insist about candidates for baptism giving a testimony to the church congregation on how they have come to faith.

On the other hand, occasional offices can be a stepping stone on an individual's journey of faith. When Alex and his wife Lucy were married in 1989 at a small rural church in Surrey, having not darkened the doors of a church for decades, they were so impressed by the gentle way in which the Rector Revd. Jeremy Cresswell led the service that they decided that they would attend church on Sundays in London thereafter. Eventually this led to them attending St Albans, Tokyo where they both came to faith on the first Alpha course run there. The rest is history!

Alex conducted one wedding for a couple, Mike and Kelly who lived outside the parish (about 20 minutes away) after requiring them to attend church 'regularly' for six months to qualify for their wedding. Generally, such couples are never seen again after their day. Alex was astonished to see them in church on the Sunday immediately after their wedding and they have been attending ever since and now run the parish's youth group, UTX.

Annual Events In addition to occasional offices, in Itchen Valley Parish, Alex organises two events a year which provide an opportunity to engage with those who do not attend church services regularly, but whom Alex has got to know during the course of the year. When casting the Way of the Cross (aka 'the Martyr Worthy Passion' – a costume drama of Christ's passion up Church Lane from the River Itchen, ending in a service at Martyr Worthy church) and Carols in the Barn (where there is a tableau of the Nativity), Alex tends to start first with those in the hinterland of the parish, rather than regular church goers. Those who are on the edges tend to appreciate being cast as Roman soldiers, those who are church attenders tend to appreciate being cast as disciples. It is only as he gets desperate (as the date draws closer and closer) that he asks followers to take part. These events draw people into the life of the church in a way which is not threatening, and they become part of the church without noticing that they are doing so! As we get to know them better it becomes reasonable to invite them to an Alpha course with integrity.

Graveyards If we come from a city or suburban church, we are unlikely to have experienced an open graveyard. Although nothing really beats a Christian burial after a funeral service (the rush of a cremation to ensure that the next service is not kept waiting sometimes feels like the life of the deceased has not been properly honoured), it is when it comes to memorial stones that the real trouble begins. It is difficult enough explaining the arcane rules of the Church of England to brides and grooms in the run up to weddings, but when families are distraught with grief, it becomes nigh on impossible. However much the individual bereaved is convinced that what their infant would most have wanted is to have a large pink teddy engraved on the gravestone, this is not possible. The best approach is to have the Diocesan and Parish rules on graveyards clearly linked on the Parish website and to include what the PCC's policy on burials and interments is, so that these can be read quietly by the bereaved before asking for any particular arrangement.

CHAPTER TEN

The relationship with the local school and youth work in the rural parish

The relationship with the local primary school has been very important in Alex's parish. Itchen Abbas Primary School is not an Anglican foundation, but the staff have been very cooperative, inviting us to conduct assemblies and also wanting to use our reordered church for many of their seasonal services and end of year ceremonies. The relationship is key because otherwise the relationship with mother and child which begins at the Little Rainbows toddlers group gets lost, particularly if the child does not choose to attend Sunday school.

One wonderful bonus of the relationship with the school has been the establishment of a youth group built around those who were in the same year at the primary school but are now at different secondary schools. The parents are keen that they maintain their friendships. UTX, as the group is called, has around 12 members between 11 and 16. There is a social event one Sunday evening a month (games, movie or cooking) including a five minute 'God slot' in which the topics for discussion are selected by the teenagers themselves – on the basis 'If you could ask God one question and knew he would give you an answer what would it be?'. Alex found that the level of theological understanding in this group was much higher than he had expected. When discussing how could a good all-powerful God allow suffering to exist and unpacking the reasoning given to him at Theological College, one of the teenagers said 'So you mean the Free Will Theodicy'? Alex found himself paddling rather fast under the surface…

In addition to the UTX social event, Alex's parish also holds a UTX Sunday Group on another Sunday once a month. UTX are currently doing Youth Alpha in this period. This has been very popular.

The main rule in dealing with school assemblies is: 'Don't be boring!' They don't really need theology. They really need to know that you can be trusted and that going to church would be fun.

If the church is a church school, there will be a requirement for the Rector (ex officio) to be a foundation governor and this will give a say in the selection of other foundation governors of the school. Selecting people to be governors who are good at committees or on education is a temptation, but actually the most important criteria is whether the person concerned is good at managing relationships. Select someone who is good at fostering that relationship between church and school.

Even if you have a secular school, there will probably be a lot of interest in the Rector being a governor. It's a great way in to one of the most important communities in the Parish.

CHAPTER ELEVEN

How to run a Rural Parish

Leadership

Leadership and management are not the same thing[13]. Rural churches need leaders and pastors. Rural Archdeacons may want managers. So, Rectors do need to be able to be all three as a minimum. Of course, none of us are equally good at each of these disciplines. We tend to emphasise the area we find most comfortable. But we need to be able to do all three. There is no doubt that if villagers can choose, they will choose a good pastor rather than anything else. Thus, many rural rectors concentrate on the pastoral. But, in fact, the rural church needs innovative leadership, if it is to grow. Creativity and risk taking are necessary.

Revd. Dr. Michael Volland, the principal of Ridley College Cambridge (who spoke at the 2017 Winchester Diocesan Synod Conference) says 'I would swap any number of 'pastors' for a good church entrepreneur'. Entrepreneurs create and build the future (as co-workers with God). Entrepreneurs create environments where anything can happen rather

13. John C.Maxwell The 21 *Irrefutable Laws of Leadership*, p13

than presiding over environments where nothing can happen. Rural churches need people who have ideas, who are going to inspire others to buy into them and who enable other people with ideas to bring them to fruition.

Often entrepreneurs are not the same sort of people who are good at managing implementation of Diocesan policies on buildings, finance, weddings and safeguarding. But however popular a Rector is (and inspirational leaders will be popular) if they cannot keep their hand on the detail of finance, weddings and safeguarding, in particular, they could easily end up having a visit from the local police, not to mention the Archdeacon and Bishop. Parishes run by overstretched Rectors are a potential recipe for unintentional (but possibly reckless) fraud and criminality.

As we have already said above, Rectors must be good pastors if they are going to be able to preach in a way which hits the spot in the community. Nothing can do more damage to a Rector's reputation in a community if he is thought not to be willing to do his share of pastoral visiting. We just cannot spend all our time locked up in our office, however many emails from the Diocese and the parish we are receiving daily. Alex tends to do pastoral visits on one or two Tuesdays a month. He travels round on his bicycle. He does not make appointments and if they are in, he visits and (if they would like to do so) offers home communion and if they are not in, then they tend to miss out until the next month.

Pastoral visiting can be incredibly emotionally demanding, particularly when you are having to deal with someone's marital problems, mental health issues or domestic abuse. We can probably all think of twenty people who would benefit from a regular pastoral visit. The problem is that it tends to be the first thing that gets lost from the diary when the Rector is under a lot of pressure.

There are two things that a Rector can do to free his time up. Firstly, he needs to establish a really good team of pastoral visitors. In Itchen Valley the team is called the 'Valley Visitors'. The team is commissioned annually and agrees to keep informational confidential and follow guidelines in their visiting. Now a team like this needs someone who is willing to co-ordinate it, but it doesn't necessarily need to involve just followers of Christ. There will be many in the rural communities in which we serve who will be willing to visit the lonely and infirm. But they may not be willing or able to pray with them or to study the Bible with them. Alex went through one phase of thinking that unless pastoral visitors pray, then the person being visited doesn't necessarily know that they have been visited by the church. However, that does not mean that we cannot cooperate with those who would not see themselves as followers of Christ in carrying out this good neighbourly activity. Provided it is co-ordinated well, pastoral visiting can be done under the Church's umbrella of insurance, training and safeguarding even by people whose faith is not as deep as we hope it will eventually become. The key to this however is that the Pastoral Co-ordinator knows what is going on, knows who is being visited, finds out who is being missed and directs the right visitor to the right person. All the pastoral visitors need to be trained to recognize when the person they are visiting has a spiritual need and is not just experiencing loneliness. In that case the Pastoral Co-ordinator will send someone who is able to meet that need, who may be a member of the clergy or a Licensed Lay Minister or a follower who is willing to pray with them. Also, the Pastoral Co-ordinator should be able to direct who wants to receive Holy Communion at home to be delivered either by a lay person trained to do this or by a member of the clergy. Bentley, Froyle and Binsted have an Anna Chaplain who makes a considerable difference to the care for the elderly in their community.

Secondly, the Rector ideally needs at least a half time paid administrator (in addition to a part time paid book keeper of which more below). Having a paid administrator is possibly more important than having a paid Rector! There needs to be someone who can pick up and action the huge number of administrative tasks in the modern church and filter the barrage of emails and telephone calls the Rector receives and which keep him from being able to engage with the community he is there to serve. Half the job of a Parish Administrator is being a PA to the Rector and half the job is being an administrator and these are not the same thing. Some time ago Christianity magazine featured the working partners of many Christian leaders – the article suggested that we would not even have heard of these great leaders without the support of their 'working partners' making everything happen for them. The gift of administration was recognised even in the first century in 1 Corinthians 12:28! It's very important. However, at £10,000 to £15,000 per annum, this may be unrealistic financially for many multi church benefices and create horror at the PCC, even if the suggestion is made. But a Rector has only so much time in his day and every hour spent doing something which could be done by a lay person more efficiently will take him away from the sermon preparation and pastoral visiting that PCCs are so keen that he should do. Also, the most recent Church of England report on Shaping Strategies for Growth (referring to the publication Released for Mission) shows that one of the characteristics associated with growth involves a 'redirection of time and energy, particularly but not exclusively for clergy, from administration and building maintenance to outreach, service and evangelism'.

Safeguarding alone has placed a colossal burden on rural churches in recent years. It has to be done right. Clergy have been sent to gaol for wedding registration irregularities. Safeguarding and weddings have to be done correctly. Legislation on data protection (GDPR) looks as if it will impose similar burdens on the clergy. This is not to mention the returns which need to be completed, the newsletters which need publishing, the rotas and meetings which need organizing. In many respects whether a rural parish can handle these burdens effectively is a litmus test of whether it should remain as an independent organisation. It would not be surprising if a Diocese wanted to merge parishes together to a level which would ensure the discharge of these statutory obligations. It is difficult to see how any Rector can be expected to do their missional task in the community with these burdens as well. Paying someone to carry out these tasks means that the Rector has at least one person upon whom he can entirely rely who will just get on with the job come what may, because volunteers are wonderful, but can be tricky...

Volunteers

Managing volunteers is not at all like managing employees. John C. Maxwell in his book The 21 Irrefutable Laws of Leadership argues that leading volunteers is the most challenging of all possible leadership situations. He writes: '[In volunteer organisations] there is no leverage. In other organisations the person who has position has incredible leverage. In the military, leaders can use rank and, if all else fails, throw people into the brig. In business bosses have tremendous leadership in the form of salary, benefits and perks. Most followers are pretty cooperative when their livelihood is at stake.

But in voluntary organisations the thing that works is leadership in its purest form: influence. Psychologist Harry A. Overstreet observed, 'The essence of all power to influence lies in getting the other person to participate.' Followers in voluntary organisations cannot be forced to get on board. If the leader has no influence with them, then they won't follow.' Maxwell suggests that the way to find out the best leaders in a commercial organisation is to ask them to lead a volunteer organisation for six months. Being successful in leading volunteers is 'the mark of true leadership' according to Maxwell.

A Rector used to a team of paid church employees may find this a difficult adjustment to make. Volunteers need to be inspired, thanked and noticed. They operate on the fuel of thanks but, most importantly, need to know that what they are doing is actually noticed by the Rector, especially if they are not yet followers of Christ. They also they need to be inspired. They need leadership and an exciting vision of the future to be presented to them. One of the striking features of Relationship Central at HTB is how Nicky and Sila Lee are constantly thanking and inspiring the volunteers that help them. Of course, thanks need to be sincere (as it is with them) and not cursory. Maxwell suggests that influence is affected by the character, relationships, knowledge, intuition, experience, past success and ability of the leader[14]. All of these things will have a bearing on whether or not the Rector has influence

14. Maxwell, Op. cit. page 17

over his parishioners.

Volunteers need to be asked and need to feel special. It is no good putting out announcements at the Parish Communion 'would anyone like to do this job?'. We need to identify someone we think has the skills and approach them individually with the request. Volunteers need to feel that they are on the inside track, part of the team, and have been recognized as having a particular skill set. No volunteer wants to be just the 'middle aged helper' (as one self-supporting curate described it). If we want to get the best out of them, we will seek to inspire them, make them feel that they are part of the team, in on what the Rector's vision is for the parish. It is no good simply delegating the jobs to them that we don't want to do as Rector. Let them know that they are appreciated and are making a genuine difference!

It may be that it is getting more difficult to persuade people to do the volunteer jobs that the church needs to be done if it is to operate at all. Millennials (and the generation before) seem busier and less keen to do these jobs than the Baby-Boomer generation. There is a reluctance to commit to anything perhaps driven by a fear of missing out on other opportunities which may come up. So, we have to up our game in asking them. Again, this is a question of being able to present an exciting picture of what doing this job will involve, the impact it will have over the generations and the immense satisfaction of a job well done. In some cases, we need to remember to commission them publicly to do the job and in all cases to pray for them in doing it.

In our planning we need to 'Start with the volunteers'. If we simply cannot get anyone to do a particular task which is part of our strategy, then it is possible that God is not blessing the plan and we may need to return to our knees to work out what do to next and even postpone that aspect of the vision for the parish for another time.

Equally, sometimes volunteers are guided by God to do things which are not on the Rector's 'to do list' and we just have to allow God the space to fire them up and let Him lead them in the direction He wants to take them. Alex preached a sermon on Peter walking on the water (largely cribbed from John Ortberg's book 'If you want to walk on water you have to get out of the boat'). There was a particular refrain every few minutes: 'But it was time to get out of the boat'. The talk went down like a lead balloon at the BCP service and was received warmly, but without much comment, at the Parish Communion. The evening service was a Taize service and Alex thought that this talk just wouldn't work in the round – better spoken from the pulpit – but went ahead with it anyway. When he had finished, (as often with his preaching) he felt embarrassed and useless – a key tactic of the enemy.

However, a lady came up to him afterwards and said, 'I have been thinking I need to get out of the boat for some months now'. So, Alex replied 'Let's meet and pray about this'. He was very excited about this opportunity, because he had a whole list of things which needed doing, particularly in the area of children and youth ministry, which was a particular priority for the parish at the time. When they met, Alex (only just) managed to keep his mouth shut and say, 'What do you feel that God is calling you to do?'. She replied, 'It's something to do with the bereaved'. God had placed this upon her heart. So, Alex introduced her to Jane Oundjan who has been running the Bereavement Journey at HTB for many years. A few months later this lady ran that course in the parish. The brilliant thing was that she took complete responsibility for the course – it was her thing and she organized it all. Just wonderful. God was working in her life and in the lives of those who attended. But this could all have been completely snuffed out if Alex had insisted that she followed his own list of priorities.

We need to see our volunteers as the ministries of the church. It is so easy to say, 'Well our church has such and such ministry to young people…such and such ministry to our senior citizens etc', whereas in fact all we have is Jane Smith who runs the youth group Mark Smith who leads the Band, John White who runs the Sunday School and Julia White who runs the seniors lunch. Losing the Whites or the Smiths can mean the loss of those ministries altogether as there may be no-one to replace them. We need to look after our volunteers and ensure that what they are doing is spiritually rewarding for them.

Volunteers need to be given room to do what God is calling them to do. Alex and Lucy are only Christians because of the generous disposition of the vicar of St Alban's Tokyo Father Bill Hargett who let Canadian Revd. (now Bishop) Jenny Andison run the Alpha Course at his church in the 1990s rather than insisting on something which suited his own churchmanship.

Focal ministers

Archbishop Justin Welby has said that 'Any church that leaves things to the "professionals" is committing missionary suicide…the responsibility of demonstratinginwordandworkstheloveofJesusChrist, in a way that is deeply attractive is the responsibility of every single Christian. Always. Everywhere'[15]. In his book 'What makes churches grow', Revd. Bob Jackson argues that every community[16] needs an individual who is the focal point of Christian mission in that community. He critiques previous attempts in rural areas to band huge numbers of different communities together in team ministries which lead to a series of little-known individuals conducting services who

15. See https://www.premier.org.uk/News/UK/Justin-Welby-Leaving-evangelism-to-professionals-is-missionary-suicide as quoted in *Shaping Strategies for Growth*

16. Whether you see an individual village as a community or a group of villages as a single community will depend upon the circumstances. A combined multi-church parish can do a lot to give several villages a sense of belonging to a single community. In the case of a single community only one focal minister would be necessary.

have no day to day engagement in the community and thus lead to declining church populations. He says that no clergyperson can meaningfully relate to a congregation of more than 120[17]. What is needed he suggests is a 'focal minister' who can be either lay or ordained, paid or unpaid and would live in that community and thus be committed to it for the long term: A person whose character is exemplary and to whom people will turn when they face difficulties in their lives and who invests in relationships with the whole hinterland of the community and not just those who attend the church. A church led by such a person has every chance to grow but we need to find many of them to cover each of our communities. Empowering others to learn to lead thus becomes a key task for the rural Rector.

There are a number of challenges with this excellent approach to rural ministry. One is the limitations of canon law on what lay people can or cannot do in church leadership. Clearly, they cannot lead communion in Anglican churches, but also there is a limitation on what they can do in terms of preaching or leading of services. Only Licensed Lay Ministers can preach and lead non-Eucharistic services regularly, unless they have the written agreement of the Bishop. In addition, in Winchester Diocese regular worship leadership is possible for those who have been given

17. Jackson, Bob, *Hope for the Church*, (London: CHP, 2002), p.121

the Bishops Commission for Mission in the discipline of leading worship, and from 2019, regular preaching is possible if they have received the Bishops Permission to Preach (after a similar, but longer, course to the BCM). Increasingly, Alex is thinking that some kind of Ordained Local Ministry is needed to fill the gap – perhaps older people with exemplary character who do not need so much formation or on whom (given their age) attempts at formation might be wasted! The dog collar still carries a lot of significance in rural communities, but the locals tend not to look beyond it as to whether a vicar is self-supporting or an incumbent; whereas the question for a lay focal minister will be 'Do they really know what they are doing?'.

A further question is what does 'community' mean in this context. Of course, one could aim for a focal minister for every village, but this may in practice mean one of the churchwardens taking on (in addition to all their heavy responsibilities for the fabric of the church building) responsibility for leading and preaching as well. Perhaps a better approach would be to have a focal minister for each community of churches in a local area (which could be a single parish multi church benefice or a multi parish benefice – see Chapter 12: Moving from a Multi Parish Benefice to a Single Parish Benefice.

Canon law does need to catch up with the needs on the ground in this area. Yet while the glacial developments in canon law take place, there is an interim solution. In Winchester Diocese (and perhaps elsewhere) the rules on Authorisation of Ministries indicate that 'Any other person asked by the priest in charge' can 'occasionally' preach or lead a non-eucharistic service. 'Occasionally' is defined to mean 'No more often than once every three months'. In Itchen Valley Parish as we have two main non-eucharistic services a month in Itchen Valley Parish – All Age Worship and Valley Worship – we could actually have as many as six potential lay ministers in training each either preaching or leading three times a year.

One of the key challenges is how to ensure a good working relationship between the focal minister and whoever has legal responsibility for the parish. If the focal minister is ordained (even though remunerated only on a half stipend or house for duty basis or even a self-supporting minister) Alex understands that there is no legal reason why that minister cannot be the incumbent of the parish with full legal responsibility and authority in that parish. However, some may take the view that this is a lonely furrow to plough and that she would be better off as part of a team ministry (with all the back up and support of ministerial colleagues) reporting to an incumbent in another nearby parish. The difficulty with this is that this means that the latter is responsible for the vision and is the chair of the PCC and APCM but does not live with and have an intimate relationship with, the people being served. A better approach might be to leave the legal responsibility with the focal minister and arrange for pastoral support from a full-time rural dean who does not have responsibility for a parish himself and thus can dedicate his entire time to looking after the focal ministers in the Deanery and ensuring that they have the support and counsel that they need to avoid being isolated. Surely the means for clergy to be supported in a Deanery is through Deanery Chapter.

In any event, as we move increasingly to needing more and more lay and self-supporting people to run the church in our communities, to become focal ministers, we need to get better and better about starting people on their spiritual journeys. Alex and his wife Lucy started running the Marriage Course in their first rural parish in which they lived as relatively new Christians. They had absolutely no idea that this would possibly lead to being called to ordination. Perhaps that is what can happen when we give spiritual significance to whatever we do, when we are doing it for the Kingdom, even making drizzle cake can have eternal significance and can start a journey which ultimately leads to church leadership!

Churchwardens, PCCs and APCMs

The importance of the relationship between the Rector and Churchwardens cannot be underestimated. She cannot do her job without their support and encouragement. It is worth taking the time to get to know them well and to keep them briefed on the developing vision for the Parish. They need to be at the inner core, her most trusted friends who will support him to the villagers and be willing to tell her where she is going astray.

The difficulty is the number. In rural churches there will probably be two churchwardens per church – so in a united benefice of six churches – twelve people. Getting them all together at any time is going to be difficult. If possible, we should try and reduce our Standing Committee to one churchwarden from every church and meet at least once a month if not more often. Entertain them at home. Become friends with them as much as is possible. They should never be in a position where they are surprised to be told by someone in the community what the Rector has said or done. They should be entirely in agreement with the Rector on what the policy is in every situation and should be able to explain it to villagers when they bring it up.

A PCC needs firm but gentle guidance. There is nothing more frustrating to anyone who has sat on a PCC than to hear the same old discussion about 'the cupboard under the stairs' being spoken about for meeting after meeting. A Rector needs to be firm about agenda items (only items notified 24 hours in advance) and needs to exercise chairmanship skills to make sure that those who are contributing are sticking to the subject. It is always astonishing for those who are still in employment that some PCC members seem to see meetings as a social or pastoral opportunity: to tell stories, nervously laugh about things which are not funny and complain about minor issues etc as the clock ticks towards 10pm and everyone wants to get home.

Being well prepared and being firm (but kind) in chairmanship should resolve this issue but needs to be done so from the outset. Take meetings seriously!

So far as elections at APCMs and correct practice are concerned, we cannot assume that simply because something is procedurally correct, that it is the right thing to do in the context of the rural church. This is a real danger for those whose professional background is the law. In particular, it's very important not to try to use worldly means to achieve what we might feel are Godly objectives.

Alex made a serious mistake in one parish. One of the challenges of the rural church is that membership of PCCs is often not at all selective. There are so few volunteers in any individual village that anyone who wants to stand as a member of the PCC, is automatically elected. It can become a dictatorship of the available and, sometimes, the least suitable. In a multi-church parish (in other words where the parishes of several villages have merged into a single parish) the pool of potential PCC members is wider than in one of the villages of an (unmerged) multi parish benefice. This means that in the case of an unmerged benefice there are seldom contested elections to join the PCC of a rural church. In the PCC concerned, there was an individual who Alex felt was so difficult that Alex used to wake up in the middle of the night thinking: 'I should have said this…or I should have said that.' Alex found dealing with this individual to be considerably more stressful than anything that he was doing at his job in the City of London at the time! So, thinking like a lawyer, Alex decided to ensure that at the next APCM there was at least one more candidate than available places on the PCC. The contested election took place, but had the unexpected result that two people (including the individual concerned, but one entirely unintended victim) came equally last and both withdrew from the election, very upset. The reverberations of this decision caused a rift in the village which lasted for years and set back the gospel in the community for a long time. Any number of apologies could not turn the clock back. This was all particularly galling because the person concerned said to Alex after the APCM 'I was going to resign anyway'. We need to recognize the pastoral significance of the decisions we take, however correct procedurally. Reflecting on this sorry tale by reference to Abram and Sarai's experience with Hagar and Ishmael in Genesis 16, Alex has seen learned that manipulation can play no part in establishing the Kingdom of God.

Finance

Getting on top of the parish finances will be a key

priority for any Rector. It's so important that there is a balance in the support for the parish across the church population, not just the older members, as it can cause a huge resentment of the younger members who may not realise that giving regularly is what they are expected to do. One of the joys of having disciples in your rural church is the generosity with which they give, often quite out of all proportion to those of the regular church attenders who are villagers but not really followers of Christ.

There is a great debate on whether the Rector should know who gives and how much. Of course, there is the danger of bias towards the bigger givers, but on the other hand many of the key new relationships will have been formed by the Rector and she will be the only person who can possibly approach them for regular support.

It is the objective of any Parish Treasurer to try and ensure that regular giving covers all regular expenses and that fund raising is only done for new projects or for charitable contributions. The fabric of the churches should be paid for by the community and the mission of the Parish should be paid for by the worshippers. This is a good balance if you can achieve it. One of the advantages of the rural church is that people do want to support their church building – it is a prized asset in the community – even if they never attend a church service. There is a distinction between giving in the context of discipleship and fund raising which is something else. The temptation for PCCs is, say, when money gets tight to tell the Rector 'Preach on giving' and there is no problem with this, but we should not preach on giving to fund raise.

Many villagers may be disposed to give to support the fabric of the church buildings but show a strange reluctance to support the Parish itself. It is for this reason that 'Friends of St Aloysius church' bodies are formed. The donors to these bodies can give entirely selfishly (if that is not a tautology) – there is no risk of the money being used by the church for anything other than the building in their own village. As mentioned above, the difficulty is that many of these bodies are often not charities and thus gift aid payments are not possible (although they would be if given to the PCC). Also, the committee can constitute yet another power base in the village with whom the Rector has to deal to get things done.

As we have seen, not everyone in the community rushes to contribute money to the church and sometimes we have to spell out to them the consequences of failing to do so. When Alex was Treasurer of Kilmeston PCC, he used villager motivations to obtain financial support for the Church from those who did not attend its services in the following way. He used to say: 'Do you want there to be a church still here for your daughter to get married in? If so, you need to contribute your share of the cost of running the church; feel free to give what you think is appropriate' and then Alex would give a range of contributions taking into account the number of households in the community, the relative size of the individual's house and the Parish Mission Fund obligations of the PCC.

Communication

Communication seems on the surface quite an easy thing: send a few emails, hand out a pew sheet and set up a website. But, actually, it is much more complex than it appears on the surface, because everyone is different. Multiple communities and multiple congregations create serious difficulties. They are different in the way that they receive information; it's partly a generational thing: do you communicate via Facebook, for 40 to 50 year-olds, or by What'sApp and Instagram, for the missing generations. You are speaking to lots of different interested parties, some of whom (depending upon the nature of the relationship that you have with them) may be misappropriating the information that you are giving them. Communication is increasingly professional in one sense. They expect information to come out instantly. From a technical point of view, Yann says, this has been the hardest thing to do during the time that he has been Rector. He had had more complaints about communication than anything else. Who do you consult, when, is a real problem particularly where you have a multiplicity of PCCs? You want to announce something and get on with it but there may not be a PCC meeting soon enough. A great advantage of a single parish benefice!

If you are part of a growing rural church, this can be a problem because you go from everyone knowing everything, to not knowing. People sometimes express disappointment in not knowing about funerals and such events.

In Itchen Valley there is the huge advantage of a really well produced Parish Magazine called Itchen Valley News – with colour photography and well edited and a number of excellent columns. The church is invited to take part in this excellent publication. But, also, we have the wonderful 'Itchen List'. This is a database of email addresses of people who live in Itchen Valley, which can automatically send an email to all 500 members (one for every household in the community) but the individual email addresses are kept confidential.

We try hard not to over use the Itchen List and thus cause annoyance to the members (there are clearly stated guidelines). However, it does mean that we can advise most of the community about deaths and thanksgiving services and also when the church is starting a new initiative. We had a very civilised debate on the Itchen List a few years ago on what would be an appropriate thing to say on the List about a bereavement and what sort of permission should be sought from the family.

Clearly, all communications will need to come within the purview of the new data-protection legislation and this will be a particular challenge for rural churches as numerous people keep email lists.

CHAPTER TWELVE

Moving from a multi parish benefice to a multi church parish

Why would you merge parishes? Surely there cannot be anything more daunting or even depressing for a potential candidate to a rural benefice to see on the parish profile that there are four or more PCCs for which she must take responsibility? The relationship with one PCC can be a challenge in itself. But the massive duplication of church officers: churchwardens, deanery synod representatives, safeguarding officers, data protection officers, treasurers, PCC secretaries and electoral roll officers for a total church population of only 200, and all the meetings involved (as the Rector has to attend all the PCC meetings and all the APCMs) is enough to make anyone blanch, but the thought of having to persuade more than one group of fairly conservative people of any change in policy, is enough to make any Rector lose the will to live. The result, of course, is that change doesn't happen. It's just easier to continue to spin the plates, to keep the show on the road, and just keep going, making no change at all. As one city evangelical vicar said to Alex 'why on earth would you want to put yourself through that?'.

And yet rural ministry can be so rewarding, as we see God act, that we want to do it. But rural church communities do need to understand that, if they want to attract good candidates, they need to organise themselves in a way which makes them easy to manage.

Hence, some benefices have transitioned into single parish benefices even though they may comprise several villages. But the struggle to achieve this change can be painful both for the local community and for the minister concerned.

But why create a single parish?

The first advantage of a single parish is the creation of a sense of common purpose and mission amongst the leadership of the benefice.

There are both spiritual and practical aspects to this:

From a spiritual perspective, God blesses churches which are in unity – it's as if we cannot bear the weight of the glory He wants to impart to us, when we are divided. This makes sense. As we know, it is the Holy Spirit who changes hearts and inclines us to want to become followers of Christ, so if we grieve or quench the Holy Spirit (Ephesians 4:30-31 and 1 Thessalonians 5:19) by conflict between Christians, then the likelihood of having a growing church is reduced. The opportunity for disagreement in a multi-parish benefice must be greater than in a single parish, as in a single parish, all the representatives have a responsibility for the whole parish. A united church receives the fruitfulness of the blessing of the presence of the Holy Spirit (Psalm 133) as He is able to transform the world around it and through it. Also, our unity is a sign to the world that He has sent us (John 17:20).

From a practical perspective, when the villages come together as one parish, with one legal representative body, and importantly one set of accounts, eventually the village representatives stop only thinking about themselves and their own village. The representatives get to know each other and as they become friends, they start to trust each other. They themselves start to worship at each other's churches and not just at their own. Eventually they see themselves as one, not, say, four, bodies.

Second, a merger enables change to happen. There is no longer a need to have months of delays as individual PCCs are consulted on everything proposed at the Benefice Council.

Third, it reduces the duplication of Churches Officers: Safeguarding, Data protection, treasurers, secretaries, electoral roll officers, thus regulatory issues are more professionally managed (less risk of decisions without faculties).

Fourth, a merger centres power in one place, rather than diffusing it in a series of unmanageable small groups, which are less demanding to deal with for clergy.

Fifth, a merger means less process which means more time for mission. Precious volunteer time is not wasted on process and can be directed towards mission.

Sixth, a merger can facilitate a reduction in low attended services without undermining over all church attendance or engagement between villagers and the church. In an important conversation to kick off negotiations for the reduction of regular services across the Parish from three per Sunday to two, one more conservative member of the PCC said to Alex 'Well it's a single parish….!' It was a very good start to a difficult discussion. Ultimately, the single PCC agreed the reduction in services without a murmur, a result which just would not have been possible if we had to take the same decision to four PCCs.

Seventh, it is easier to recruit clergy for appointments.

But are there any disadvantages to a single parish benefice?

Firstly, a merger of Parish does risk losing engagement with the community in smaller villages. It's very important to ensure that there are enough regular services in the smaller less well attended villages to motivate the villagers to keep them engaged (acting as Churchwardens, looking after the building and contributing to the Common Mission Fund).

Secondly, it's hard work to set up – a merger can easily be de-railed by even one small community and so it needs strong episcopal leadership and probably the leverage of a new appointment to happen.

Can't the same result be achieved by another means? One of the benefices in Winchester Diocese has come up with an ingenious way of creating a 'virtual' single parish by what it calls its 'Benefice Forum'. To reduce the huge number of meetings, all the PCCs in the benefice are held in the same building at the same time. The matters common to all of them are held together and then business which relates only to individual parishes is then discussed in separate rooms. While this is a very good option if a merger cannot be achieved (and may be a good staging post on the way to merger ultimately), it does not achieve the principal aim, which is the sense of common purpose and mission. This is clear as soon as any discussion of money comes up. When the question of whether one parish will support another parish which does not have enough money to make the repairs required by the Quinquennial Architects Inspection, the result can be fireworks! But it's not just about money, getting inter parish co-operation on services (so that the precious volunteer time is not squandered in a multiplicity of small efforts for, say, ministry for children or youth in each of the villages, rather than managed in one of the villages best placed to conduct that mission) is a huge challenge. With a single parish benefice, because there is one Christingle, one Carols in the Barn, one crib service etc to which all four villages are invited and representatives from all four villages are involved, people meet each other across the villages and become friends.

Then there is the multi layered cake issue. If you

imagine a cake with several different layers represents the entire population of a rural benefice, there will be at least three different churchmanships within that benefice – evangelical, catholic, liberal/traditional. If you cut the cake in the regular way from centre to the outside then this is like how a multi church benefice is organised: a few of the evangelicals, a few of the Catholics, a few of the liberals in each village church.

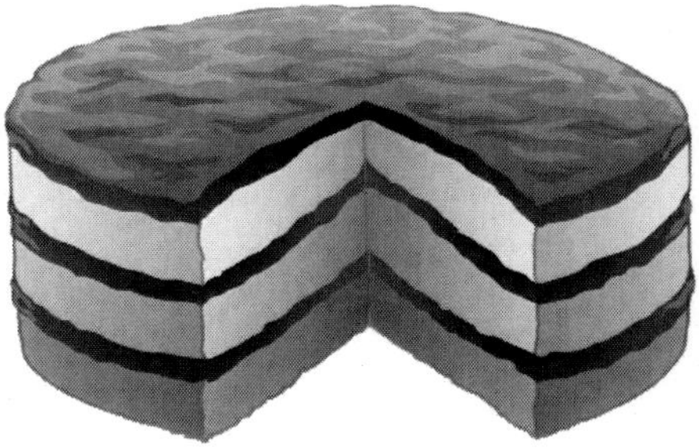

However, if you cut the cake layer by layer, you have all the evangelicals, all the Catholics, all the liberals. A single parish enables you to specialise in particular forms of worship in the church buildings most suited for that type of worship. So, for example, the charismatics can concentrate on the one reordered church building in the single parish rather than be constantly wanting to remove the pews from the church in 'their village church'. Equally, if one church building is particularly suited for contemplative worship and say Sung Evensong then that this the place that specialises in that. This avoids duplication of effort, maximises the use of the energy of the different forms of spirituality in the combined community and actually reduces potential conflict between all of those who should be working together for the kingdom in the community.

How do you organise a single parish? There has to be a scheme (under Rule 18 of the Church Representation Rules 2011 and in accordance with the Pastoral Measure 1983). This must be approved by either an Annual Parochial Church Meeting or an Extraordinary Parochial Church Meeting by a two thirds majority of the combined parish. The scheme will provide for the creation of districts within the parish corresponding to the constituent parishes of the combined parish. Each District then has a District Church Council and a District Church Meeting corresponding to the PCC and APCM which it would have had before the merger and election for these bodies goes ahead as if they were PCCs and APCM with two Churchwardens being appointed for the combined Parish from the individual districts. Also, changes to the Church Representation Rules in 2020 will make the move from a Benefice Forum to a body with legal powers to hold property much easier.

However, the real difference comes in the districts' powers. The district has no power to manage money or hold property. The management of the church building and church yard, the provision of necessaries and staffing for worship at that church and fund raising in the district for the combined parish are the primary responsibilities of the DCC. All decisions about styles of worship, liturgy, services, mission are all decided by the PCC of the combined parish. The Rector need not attend most of the meetings of the DCCs although is required to attend the Annual District Church Meeting and it is advisable to attend a DCC meeting from time to time.

In addition to the Scheme there would be a non-binding policy guidance paper which addresses the following points: that the is an intention to keep the churches of the combined parish open for regular and festive worship; that the PCC will not make any major changes or alterations to a church building without the agreement of the churchwardens nominated by the relevant DCC; the DCC may make recommendations to the PCC on the use of any funds restricted to their church; and for the establishment of PCC committees to deal with finance, budgeting, management and accounting.

Doesn't a combined PCC just create another level of bureaucracy? The way to look at this is to compare what there is before to what there is afterwards. Before you have as many PCCs and Churchwardens and church officers as there are villages. Afterwards, you do have an additional layer, but as the DCCs have no real power (only responsibilities – for maintenance and fund raising) the opportunity for conflict is vastly reduced. The real time that an additional level of bureaucracy is created is when you have a Benefice

Council supervising a multiplicity of parishes. In that case, the village representatives constant refrain is 'Well I will have to go and ask my PCC' when any proposal is put forward, thus delaying anything new by weeks, if not months. Because the Combined PCC has actual power, the quality of debate is hugely improved as the more motivated are drawn to the PCC and the church's mission stops being hijacked by the preferences of difficult individuals at a village level who generally find themselves isolated if they are elected to the PCC. The community of the combined parish starts to work as those from each village get to know each other.

Can you create a single parish in any situation? There is no point trying to create a single parish between two communities which are culturally and demographically very different. There is no point in trying to create a single parish between an urban or suburban community and a rural community. But there is no reason why not to do so between rural villages. To say, as Alex has heard said, 'But we cannot merge with them, they fought on the other side during the Civil War' is just ridiculous and a mask for the personal preference of the individual church officers concerned, rather than a legitimate objection in the interests of the community.

Probably, there is no point in merging parishes if they are geographically inconveniently located. A good test is to see if the proposed merger covers the same area as the catchment area for the local primary school. There is then every chance that the parents who take children to that school will see themselves as belonging to the merged community. Another good test is, can the Rector cycle round the whole of the merged parish in a morning?

How on earth do you go about achieving the merger? Firstly, you need leadership. You need a Rector who is generally favoured by all the parishes to achieve this. It is the sort of thing that a very popular and successful Rector can do as his time in the Benefice draws to a close.

Secondly, you need to take the money seriously. The biggest obstacle tends to be concerns that St Bartholomew's (which has a large fabric fund due to many legacies over the years) is going to have to finance the profligate parish of St. Aloysius. Start with pooling Sunday collections and get parishioners used to the idea that all the money is going to one pot.

Thirdly, allow each of the villages to have a fabric fund which is not pooled and also a 'Friends of St Aloysius Fund' which stands outside the PCC and enables villagers to give to the fabric of their own particular church. Many villagers who are not followers of Christ will only be willing to contribute to a non-PCC fund. Let them do so! The disadvantage of the Friends approach is that these are not charities and thus gifts to them are not tax deductible.

Fourthly, encourage all the villages to get all the fabric work they need actioned, done before the merger – in other words spend the fabric fund to the extent this is possible.

Fifthly, get your most able church officers involved in leading the process. This is something that successful businesspeople or accountants or civil servants can lead.

Sixthly, scope out potential opponents early and go and speak to them. Show that you care about them and are not just riding roughshod over their legitimate concerns.

Conclusion

The advantages of forming a single parish are huge in terms of mission in the community in which you have been appointed as Rector. And if you find a post where the merger has already happened: don't delay, put in an application!

CHAPTER THIRTEEN

Conclusion

There can be a sense for a New Wine priest stepping down the aisle at his installation in a rural parish that he has moved not only geographically, but also in time. Few of the assumptions on how to behave in the city or suburb are applicable. Obstacles can be fallen over before you know it and he can easily find that he is not starting at zero but at minus 50 in bringing people to Christ because of something that he said or decided in his first week when he did not understand the significance of what he was doing!

The countryside is beautiful and a great contrast with the city and it is easy to say, 'How fortunate you are to be working as Rector in such a place' and that is of course true. However, rural idylls are only as good as the people who live in them. Yann and Alex are very fortunate to be in communities of very friendly and encouraging people. But it has to be said that this is not every Rector's experience in the rural church.

We hope that the thoughts put out in this short book will help a New Wine minister to navigate some of the difficulties and to have as much fun as we have in seeing God at work in a rural environment.

December 2019

APPENDIX

How I became a follower of Christ in the rural church

Tessa

I had been widowed, but was still living in the village where my husband and I lived after we were married when a new vicar was installed [Revd Bob Earnshaw]. He initiated it and came to visit me one morning. Not long into our time together he said to me 'Do you know I don't know whether you are a Christian or not?' I was very taken aback (most likely visibly but he was not the sensitive type) and experienced quite an angry reaction deep down inside. Had he not, after all seen me in church on a regular basis?

What he did not know was that many years before in London I had ceased going to the 'buzz' (evangelistic) talks in London when I first went to work there - held initially in people's homes and then in a hotel room as a result of the burgeoning fascination – because of the extreme discomfort that I had felt when someone brazenly asked me that very same question 'Are you a Christian?' Interestingly, it was the resonation that bothered me most. What, actually are they asking me? After a moment's pause and coming down on the side of honesty I replied, 'I don't know exactly what you mean by that question?' And the reply 'That tells me that you are not'. Point finale, and ... well!

If my memory serves me correctly that was pretty much the end of that encounter – I was shell shocked and the vicar a man of only a few, but always very direct words did not elaborate. (Effective!) All I know is that he had taken to leaving a few books for anyone who wanted to borrow them, in the church porch and I took and read one by Joni Eareckson (Secret Strength maybe or Glorious Intruder) – which was hugely inspirational and set me on the path to finding out a good many answers. Or perhaps more importantly fuelled my interest.

There are several things of particular note about the appointment of this vicar. He and his wife did not at all obviously fit the mould for a rural country parish in the south of England, coming from Birmingham with two young adopted and pretty rumbustious children and the wife unlike our previous vicars' wives needing to work to earn, so unable either to help the vicar a great deal, be generally available or an 'ear' in the parishes.

Shamefully, the new vicar was 'seen off' by the PCCs fundamentally because they were not doing things as they had been done in the past, and several of the most traditional routines we had been observing he was not going to compromise over. He also suggested we close a gypsy church-in-the-wood which had no electricity and he thought was a drain on resources of every sort, including manpower.

However, there are a large handful of committed Christians, still living in the community, who made their commitment thanks to him and his evangelical ministry, and have gone on with the Lord, one becoming a lay minister.

Speaking personally, it was because of his, to put it politely 'no nonsense' approach, that I first became a seeker, and I have always been convinced that he was prompted by the Lord to ask me if I was a Christian, because only He knew the significance to me of it and it and that it would take root and gird me into action.

Bruce

I became committed to Christ during the Easter of 1986 at the culmination of a Lent course in our local multiple church Benefice.

Shortly after moving into our village there was a change of Rector. The outgoing Rector and his wife were retiring and the new Rector [Revd Bob Earnshaw] was a young married man with two small children embarking on his first appointment as a priest.

There could not have been a bigger contrast in styles. The outgoing priest was a quiet pastoral man, very approachable and welcoming. He conducted services using the Book of Common Prayer and had a good regular attendance in each of the Churches in his care.

At this time my wife and I were only very occasional attendees and were not drawn to much involvement in the village.

The new priest had a very evangelical style, outgoing and busy with a desire to engage all age groups and to introduce new styles of worship into the parishes. Initially, apart from meeting him when he was out and about, we still had little to do with the church. This changed when he decided to run a Lent course. It was not the opportunity to study the Bible that caught our attention, but the location of the course on each of the evenings.

As you might expect, in this wealthy part of Hampshire, most of the villages have some very fine historic houses and they were a fascination to those of us who had moved into the countryside from a densely populated coastal town. And so fascinated were we that we could not pass up the opportunity to see the inside of these country homes with their large estates. So, it was that we enlisted in the Lent course of 1986 to see how 'the other half' lived. We were not disappointed, and enjoyed the environs of our Lent course. But, little known to us at the beginning, the material covered in the Lent course and the way it was delivered started to take a greater priority in our reason for attending. Eventually the fine houses took second place to the desire to learn more about God, Christ, the Holy Spirit and Salvation.

It transpired that our new Rector had drawn together from across the parishes a few committed Christians with very personal and inspiring stories to tell. At the end of the course my wife and I both felt that we had been touched by the Spirit and decided that we must make the commitment to follow Christ and to become more involved in the Church.

Hindsight, as they say, is a great thing and when looking back it became obvious to us that God's hand had been at work. He knew our weaknesses and desires and used them to bring us to a place where we could see the truth of the Gospel and respond.

Jesus has done immeasurable things, our lives have been transformed. We have gone from being selfish, inward looking and worldly driven people where God was at the bottom of our priorities, to people for whom God comes first, family second and everything else thereafter. We try to be witnesses to Christ in our communities and our churches in as loving a way as we can manage. Initially, we joined the bible study group that was formed in the wake of that first Lent course and learnt as much as we could about what it means to be a Christian, a follower of Christ and his word. We started attending church every week and got progressively more involved.

Our young Rector did not last long. He was encouraged to move on by those elements within the church for whom change is nasty word. He would say that he was there for as long as God had wanted him there. There is no doubt that God used him to bring a number of people to faith and into an eternal personal relationship with their Saviour.

I don't think my understanding of who Jesus is has

changed since that day I made my commitment. He is still the Son of God. He is still my Saviour and my Spiritual guide. I may know a lot more about him and what he did while he walked this earth and about the church that grew out of his death, but my fundamental and probably somewhat childish understanding is unchanged. He loves me and I love Him. I owe him everything.

Charlotte

Although I was brought up a Catholic (being baptized, confirmed and going to Church every Sunday with my mother and grandparents), I don't really remember talking about faith and a relationship with Jesus. In fact, I didn't really know much about the Bible as neither my family or myself read it! As a teenager I started to question the Catholic faith and eventually denounced my faith at around 17 or so when I met my future husband, who had no particular religious background.

My next interaction with Jesus and Christianity came when we moved to our village twenty-two years ago. It was only because our children attended the local Church of England primary school that we felt we should attend the family service occasionally. However, as my life entered a turning point with my boys becoming independent and my desire to focus on my art, I felt that I was suppressing something deep inside myself: not only my artistic side, but also my desire to be closer to God.

I had occasionally prayed to God, but it wasn't until about twelve years ago at our village church Patronal Service that I received an answer to my prayers. I had helped make up the numbers in the small church choir and we'd been asked to sing at the communion service. As I didn't know if I could take communion, given my Catholic background, I decided to go for a blessing, as all the choir went up the altar rail and I didn't want to be noticed by not going. When the vicar placed his hand on my head for the blessing, I had a spiritual experience. I felt a surge of energy escaping my body which left me in a collapsed state, leaving me trembling and crying at the altar rail. It was in this moment that I heard an authoritative, emotionless voice which was not my own. It simply said: 'I love you. Listen to him. Be yourself – as I made you.'

It was clear to me that God was pleased that I had gone to him. I felt an absolute sense of truth that everything written in the Bible had actually happened: something which I had always questioned. In that split second, an ecstatic feeling of joy and light descended over me. While I felt very vulnerable and afraid at this strange experience, I also felt peaceful – and eager to learn more about Jesus' teachings.

Looking back, I feel as though this experience set me free. Although at the time I felt extremely frightened, vulnerable and self-conscious, I found I wanted to learn more and more about the teachings of Christ:

from joining Alpha Courses to joining Home Groups and studying the Bible. I now feel as though I have a certain confidence and inner freedom, as each new experience with Jesus and the Holy Spirit strengthens my faith and brings me closer to inner peace and self-fulfilment.

To me, Jesus is now the focus of my life. I'm not perfect in any way, I often get things wrong: 'Put my foot in it' so to speak – but to me, Jesus is now central to how I try to live my life. It is not easy and I'm still a work in progress. He is my comforter, my supporter in times of trial. Although my experience is a very personal one, I now know that everything that God and Jesus teach us is real. He is my shepherd, but I can be a stubborn sheep at times as I don't always trust in Him! However, I know I'm still a work in progress and need to totally trust in Him. Even though I can't fully comprehend the enormity of His being, I know that through studying His words in the Bible and attending Church and Home Group that He is watching over me, protecting me and guiding me to the right path in life.

Matt

I wouldn't say there was a specific date as to when I first became a disciple of Christ. More so I grew in faith over a number of years, whilst attending our local youth group as an early teen. The youth group itself was run by a Christian charity who linked a number of different rural churches and the youth within the parishes of said churches. Without the youth group I'm can't say I would've attended my local church, due to its old school, traditional services that lacked any great appeal to myself. My first encounter, that I was aware of or acknowledged, with the living God was during a time of worship and prayer on our youth groups weekend away. My youth leaders prayed and invited the Holy Spirit to let His presence be known, an experience surreal to all unchurched. From that point onwards, I knew there was something more to life and naturally I wanted to know more.

It was through my youth workers' ministry and investment in me that I developed a relationship with God. I saw Jesus in them, although at the time I didn't know that's what made them so different – their attitudes towards their own lives and the lives of others. The way they treated others and put them first was what really spoke to me, perhaps due to it being the total opposite to how I'd always put myself first.

Without being too clichéd, Jesus has completely changed my life. Most importantly it's changed my attitude towards others. I want to serve and help bring forth the Kingdom, looking out for others who wouldn't have got a second thought from my younger self. I'm currently a worship intern at a church in a major city, having moved away from my home in the North to do so, and hope that I can dedicate the rest of my adult life and future career(s) to serving Jesus and His church.

Hampshire Couple

We (my wife and I) were both brought up in conventional churchgoing families, were confirmed and continued to go to church, though our understanding of what being a Christian was all about was pretty superficial. However, a new enlightened vicar of our village church in Somerset back in around 1990 sparked a desire in both of us to find out more about Christianity and this was clearly the starting point of our progression from being simply churchgoers. We attended a small bible class and the vicar drew a wonderfully simple diagram, with us at the centre of a circle. He then asked where God was on the diagram, to which we replied that He was probably near the circumference. Ever since then, we would like to think that, through bible reading and bible study, attending churches which have comprehensive teaching, plus listening to religious talks, our discipleship has steadily grown. In terms of when we got to the stage of being able to say that we fully understood what being a disciple of Jesus Christ was, that was a relatively recent development.

What made us decide to become followers? We believe that this was probably always the case, but it was very dilute in the early stages. Age, experience of life and some excellent teaching by a small group of lay people has helped to firm up our belief.

It has to be said that, until very recently, the activities and individuals in and linked to our local church have been predominantly lay led. The latter have been responsible for the burgeoning of truly family services i.e. short (30-40 minutes) and devoid of 'churchy language' but containing a good piece of teaching for the parents. Additionally, it has been due mainly to three outstanding individuals living close by that our faith has continued to move forward. The lay people started a small study group of 8 people, a number which we felt was ideal. We studied the bible and Christian books and had short prayers. For us, this was a very positive experience and not in the least daunting. The arrival of a dynamic new vicar and three curates in the benefice has given new impetus in many ways, not least a real feeling that Jesus Christ is totally relevant for all of us here today.

From my point of view, I have a very strong belief of God having provided real support, particularly in two conflicts [war zones] and in a very challenging job later on. Both of us, having developed a steadily strengthening faith, want to try and live our lives through Jesus, something which we would describe as 'work in progress'!

Martin and Karen

The process of becoming a disciple of Christ properly started with the Family Service in the village. Prior to that church had been a thing for me anyway that one did because its 'what you did'. And then I saw the family service advertised in the village magazine. We took the parish magazine because we had always taken the parish magazine wherever we lived. We thought that now that we had moved to our parish, that it would be nice to come to a family service with our young children.

We found the approach was informal. It was the enthusiasm of the lay Christian couple leading the service which made the biggest difference. They weren't part of a mad sect! That's what brought us back. Enthusiastic, relatively informal but not crazily informal – it still felt familiar – but passionately delivered, quite honestly. As quite a child (in terms of Christianity) at the time the simpler messages really brought the message home maybe than more complex illustrations. Adults don't really need a long, complicated service. Then there was the follow up to all that which was really important. The big turning point after that was when we were offered a home group. It was called 'Just wondering'. We knew a few people who were attending. Then the Christian couple went abroad.

The next turning point was being taken to a 'grown up' church – totally different experience. What we had been doing was once a month for families. And we were then introduced us to a church in the local town, which was a totally different experience for adults. So, we got there and were amazed that a church could be like that. Filled with so many lovely people and sermons that did not drive you to sleep, had a real message and the Bible was important, we were encouraged to take the Bible out of the pew and read it during the reading at the same time the Bible was referred.

I think it was in those services that I first felt the presence of God. And modern worship songs. Just great. It felt more relevant. We did Alpha quite early on. It was the first time I had been forced to think about my faith and what it really meant. It was quite challenging. I was a bit scared about being challenged. It even made me a bit uncertain. I really had to rebuild it because this thing that I felt that I had had wasn't really anything that I had experienced before. In a sense you have to take that all away and build it back up something which is more of a true foundation. It had to be there but there had to be a proper foundation. That's what Alpha did it gave me a proper foundation.

Karen: If we hadn't had faith it would not have been possible to tolerate what has happened with our children. A very tough few years. When I was consumed with the minute detail of my daughter's survival the strength of Martin's faith was very important. It would have been easy to be overwhelmed.

Tim

I became a follower of Christ in the Autumn/Winter 2002 whilst living in a small village in the [Midlands]. I had recently remarried following a painful divorce which left me carrying a metaphorical rucksack stuffed with guilt and remorse for the pain my actions had caused.

It was very much a 'come and see' experience.

My wife was working away at the time and my next-door neighbours Mike and Mary (Mike was the NSM working with David Cook) would invite me for a meal on Tuesday evenings. One such evening Mike invited me to one of David's 'God in the Pub' talks in the local pub. David was talking that night on John 4 (now my favourite chapter in the whole Bible!). I had never listened to such a real and living exposition of any part of the Bible and I was so fortunate to hear David do such a good job of it that evening. The more he spoke the more relevance that chapter had on my life; it really spoke to my condition. At the end of his talk David said a short prayer of commitment saying that if anything we had heard that night resonated with us then just say 'Amen' to the prayer. I did and felt that metaphorical rucksack shift and slip. On the way back home,I said to Mike: 'I think I just met God in the pub.'

From that evening I realised that I had been forgiven for what I had done - it didn't relieve me of the consequences of my actions; I still have my moments of remorse. I wanted to learn more about Jesus and embarked on theological studies because I felt that as a forgiven sinner I had been called to the ministry. This was not to be the case and my eager faith took a bit of a battering. Over the years I thought I had discerned a number of paths but each of them ended up as a dead end.

I was getting the institutional church mixed up with the lovely Jesus. They don't mix. Now to me Jesus is the

Beckoning One - always calling me quietly outward and onward. My preferred worship style is contemplative. I have been led to the Celtic Christian practice of the Northumbria Community where Jesus underpins everyday life in all its exciting ordinariness and where I am now working towards Companionship.

Mary

I had been visited by an American woman (a bit younger than me) who I had just met at a friend's lunch party in Newmarket. She was very up-front about being a committed Christian. She came to stay for 3 days (long story why!) and told me everything I wanted to know (but only when I asked) about Jesus, God, the Bible, Heaven and Hell, why go to church etc. and religion in general, all the usual difficult questions people have... but it was spread out over 3 days but it was only us there so plenty of uninterrupted time.

On January 21st 1990 – the beginning of 'the decade of evangelism' - in my own home, in bed at night. I prayed properly for the first time in years ... immediate feeling of calm, connection, reassurance, bathed in warmth and light and love, amazing sudden realisation that I was meeting Jesus 'face to face' - but invisible. I have never forgotten it.

Jesus means everything to me now (and even right there and right then), it has never altered and he gives me so much strength to do everything that I do for Him. I do have split second moments of doubt and then remember it all again, all the answered prayers, all the reassurance, all the guidance, all the strength which, believe me, I do not have on my own(!).

Jo

This all happened over a period of time from 1995 to 1996, when I was aged 38, and began to worship at the local parish church.

I think I had always been open to the idea of faith, but just couldn't bring myself to believe. My sister was a Christian from early teens, having been drawn in by Baptist friends at school. I went to convent schools (for educational reasons, not religious ones) and so was immersed in Catholicism through my school years. I could see that people of faith 'had something', but it all seemed illogical to me. By 1995 we had two children, both baptised out of convention, for the second baptism in 1994 our vicar had a gentle non-pushy chat with us about Christian faith. The catalyst came when the same vicar invited us to attend an Alpha course beginning January 1995. There wasn't a 'light bulb' moment, rather a gradual realisation that I did believe that Jesus was and is the Son of God, that he died for me, and rose again. I tried prayer, and felt it was answered. At the end of the course I decided to join a Bible Group, and gradually became convinced enough in my faith to want to be confirmed which happened on Palm Sunday 1996.

My faith in Jesus led me to want to worship regularly, and then to get involved in the work of the church. I began to help at further Alpha courses, to co-lead a Bible Group, to get involved in children's work such as Holiday Club, and even to participate in the planning and leadership of some services (e.g. Family Services of the Word, Crib Service, Christingle). I came to believe in the power of prayer, and often sent up little arrow prayers during the course of the day, I felt that Jesus walked with me. In 1999, again at the suggestion of the same vicar, I began studies on a Diocesan Ministry Course. After a year of study, we were invited to 'discern' whether God had a ministry in mind for us, and I felt an increasingly strong although very unwelcome calling to ordained local ministry. I battled against it for several weeks before giving in and submitting to the exploration and selection process. I was ordained in 2002, priested in 2003, and worked in my parish (subsequently benefice) as an Ordained Local Minister until early 2017 when I stepped down for health and family reasons. I am absolutely certain that Jesus called me to that ministry, blessed me in my ministry, and blessed others through my ministry.

Life has dealt a number of knocks, causing me to be very angry with God sometimes, but I have never lost my faith. There are a lot of things I don't understand, in spite of all the study I have done, but I stick with the, for me, rock solid bottom line as mentioned above – that Jesus is the Son of God, and that he died and rose again for me. That is my bedrock and is all I need to know. Because of Jesus I believe that God loves me, forgives me, wants to provide for me, and will guide me if I let him. Jesus gives me hope. I can't imagine life without faith in him. He is the treasure in the ordinary jar of clay that is me.

Sylvia

I grew up in W and regularly attended the church with the family including Sunday School, Girl Covenanters and the annual Beach Mission. I went to college as a Christian was continued to be involved in Christian activities. I had the grounding of a life in a Christian setting with the encouragement to a personal response as a young teenager following a Beach Mission.

I married at 23 and gradually drifted away from church-going. In my late 20s we moved and when a new neighbour invited our daughter to join Sunday School I started going to church with her for the monthly family service. This awakened me to the fact that something was missing. I increased my church going but didn't find the vicar and the small, ageing congregation helping to rebuild my spiritual health.

It was then I started to attend the neighbouring village church at the next-door village. This was welcoming and alive with Christian teaching and living. Through a Holy Spirit day (not part of an Alpha course) God finally brought this prodigal daughter back home. I joined a mid-week home group and a weekly prayer meeting. I have continued to grow in my Christian faith and understanding since then.

He has been totally faithful despite my wavering, denials, lack of love, anger, criticism of other Christians who made me feel uncomfortable etc new starts, forgiveness, love and encouragement, an identity that remains no matter what other experiences have made me feel insignificant. He drew me back through a series of events and people and continues to keep me in touch through the good teaching and fellowship of a Christian community. He has given me a perspective of life beyond the often depressing human perspective.

He is the source of all that is good and trustworthy, but also the challenge to my desire for independence and self-importance. When I recall the faith journey so far I know Jesus is there for me and through his Spirit will keep leading me on, will 'complete the good work he has begun' though it takes to the end of time!

Kerry

I grew up believing that I was a Christian. My dad and brother were in the choir at church. It seemed the natural thing to be confirmed and attend the AYPA. At Uni I had a couple of Christian friends and we would attend church/go the CU together.

When I left these communities, I still thought I was a Christian, but didn't attend church on any kind of regular basis.

Many, many years later, my daughter was baptised and I felt that I should give her the same kind of upbringing that I had. We started to go to our village church and 11 years later I still go (she is more erratic!). Over these years, I feel that my Christianity has 'grown'. I have been lucky to feel part of the community here and got involved on both a practical and more spiritual basis. I think what has brought me closer is groups/ meetings that I have been to outside the Sunday 'usual hours'. At present I belong to a 'book group' of supportive women. We do a variety of things together and some have really challenged what I believe and just how I should live my life (on the inside and the outside). The talking, listening and reading (things that I wouldn't choose myself) has given me space to explore and grow. Not one big event. Many different sized ones.

At the moment, I think that Jesus is my guide – giving me a model, pointers and direction on how to live. Someone who makes sure that I keep checking myself. I still wonder how much I truly believe though! Jesus is also a source of strength to me - to do what I do. To do my best. I am still on my journey.

Jan

In 2009-2010, having just retired from teaching, I had a long viral illness and was mostly confined to bed. This was a very difficult time for me and I felt full of despair. M and some of the church Elders came to visit me at home and it was during these kind visits that the conversation turned to Christ. I eventually felt drawn to give my life to Christ, joining a Home Group and later going on an Alpha Course too.

Through conversation and much prayer with my visitors, I suddenly made sense of why I had been ill at such a pivotal time in my life. Instead of feeling sorry for myself, I began to feel that I had been 'brought low' so that God could build me up again. Through prayer, I felt led back to the Bible and suddenly it was as though a veil had been lifted and I could make sense of the Old and New Testaments. Being a keen archaeology and history 'buff', I suddenly realised that the Bible is full of solid facts and proofs of events which actually happened and people who actually existed. This had a huge impact on my growing faith.

Jesus means everything to me now. I feel his presence, I know he sends His Holy Spirit to watch over us and that He is a very real presence here and now. I understand that we are His hands and feet, doing the work on the ground that He wishes us to do. For me prayer and reading the bible are a very essential part of each day. Life is not necessarily easier, but I have a spiritual purpose now and, as well as the Home Group, I am even part of a Prayer Team at church. I also feel drawn to be part of a Healing Ministry.

Jenny

I was baptised and confirmed in an active rural parish and loved going to church, but life took a different turn when I reached my early 20s. I lost my links with the Church, although I did not lose my faith.

Looking back, I would say that I did not begin to become a true follower of Christ until early 2016 -after I had been attending our local Church for about a year. However, I think the most significant point was during the Alpha course which began in January 2017.

I moved to the village during the 1980s and started to attend a monthly service in another church - often led by friends who were Readers. I also joined an 'occasional' choir serving three churches in that area and enjoyed supporting their small congregations (until my husband's health deteriorated).

When my husband died at the end of 2014 the funeral took place in our local Church and the Vicar was very helpful and supportive. A few weeks later, although I was still in a bit of a 'fog', I had a strong desire to go back to church. I had not attended our local in the past, but I was made welcome and after the service one of the Lay Elders who had known me for many years said … 'Do come back and see us again'. I went home in tears, but knew that I would return the following week.

The next Sunday service included Communion (led by Rev M), who immediately spotted me sitting with a friend and came over to ask who I was. As M gave me the bread she remembered my name, which made the first Communion I had received in a long time feel so personal and special. M and the Vicar's wife were setting up a new 'Living with Loss' group at that time, so I was encouraged to join and it became a great support to me over the next two years.

So, I continued to attend Church almost every Sunday. The Informal Service of Morning Prayer on a Wednesday (followed by a drop-in café) also gave me support and a spiritual boost. I was re-learning stories from the Bible through the many easy to follow talks and sermons, which often seemed very relevant to my life. I enjoyed taking part in all forms of worship – also the coffee and fellowship which took place afterwards! I loved the music, especially the uplifting modern worship songs.

In 2016 I was encouraged to go to the Maundy Thursday Supper, which turned out to be the beginning of an important move forward in my faith. I found the meal - interspersed with the wonderful service of shared Communion - very moving and thought provoking. I suddenly realised that Jesus had died for me personally and as I sat in the Church for the quiet period of meditation and prayer which followed, the familiar Easter story began to reveal a much deeper meaning. By coincidence, I also joined the choir from that weekend. Sitting (rather tentatively!) in the choir stalls at the local Church on Easter Morning was another big step and such a privilege.

At the beginning of 2017, Mary and other Church members encouraged me to join Alpha. I was keen to take part in this as I still had so much to learn. I found Nicky Gumbel's talks very compelling and the Leaders were able to answer our questions in ways which were easy to understand. I was learning how to build a better relationship with God, through Jesus, by more meaningful prayer and Bible reading. My understanding and faith increased as the weeks progressed, peaking on the 'Holy Spirit Day' which was the perfect setting for me to feel the spiritual presence of God – though not for the first time in my 'new life'.

The last session on that day - 'How can I be filled with the Holy Spirit?'- included the subject of 'speaking in tongues' which I thought must be amazing, but maybe not for me just yet, if at all. It was not discussed in the group. At the end of that lovely day M prayed over me to receive this Gift, although I felt a little unsure so it seemed unlikely to happen for me at that moment. I was also anxious about a relative who had been taken ill that morning, so as I returned home I concentrated my prayers on the health situation.

When good news came, nearly 48 hours later, I thanked God for answering my prayers and asked Him whether I could now receive the Gift of Tongues. I have to admit that I did not really expect anything to happen at that stage, so I was totally overwhelmed when I found myself beginning to speak in phrases I could not understand. It took me some while (with support from the Course Leaders) to take in the fact that I had been blessed with such a wonderful Gift. It was also the point at which I promised to entrust my life to Him.

Following on from Alpha, M set up a new Home Group which I was pleased to join as I still have a lot to learn. We support one another in prayer, study the Bible and discuss how the teaching of Jesus relates to our everyday lives. This gives me encouragement and I always look forward to the weekly meetings.

It helps to be able to talk to Jesus like a friend and I feel that God speaks to me through reading the Bible (using a daily guide).

I do not think that I could have coped without Him and the support of the church family. It is also rewarding for me to be involved/ help with church activities. As you can see from my story, Jesus has given purpose to life on my own and hope for the future. My only regret is that it took me so many years to reach this point! He means everything to me now.

Hugh

I became a follower instead of a passive acceptor of Jesus during and after the Alpha course. The period following was the most important to nurture and increase my depth of commitment, I am not sure my faith would have survived without this time. And that course was followed with some years as members of a weekly Bible study group. The weekly group nurtured my faith and I grew in understanding and commitment. This period I would describe as the time I moved from seeking to following.

Maggie

I went to Sunday School and church until I was a teenager, was baptized as a baby and confirmed around 13. Then I'm afraid I fell pretty much by the wayside, as do so many, attending church only very occasionally for Christmas and Easter and services for my children's school.

Fast forward until 2007 when my husband, Tony, who had been suffering with advanced cancer for 9 years became very ill indeed and was admitted to the local Hospice. He was not expected to survive, but after 3 weeks those wonderful people had stabilized him enough so that he could return home, as he so dearly wished, for what was the last 3 weeks of his life. I was lucky enough to be able to stay by his side for that time in the Hospice and during that time had had some chats with the Chaplain who was a great comfort and support to me. Indeed, he was kind enough to give the Eulogy at Tony's funeral; which was very good of him considering my husband would not talk to him, although I very much wanted him to!

A couple of months after Tony died M contacted me to say she and S (an elder) were starting up a new Living with Loss Group which I attended. M, S and the Hospice Chaplain impressed me so much with their obvious faith and kindness that I thought there must be something I've missed out on here. So I then joined a Home Group and have been on one pretty consistently ever since. Early on I also went on an Alpha course and learned a lot (although I must admit the Holy Spirit and speaking in tongues session rather freaked me out at that time!) - I have got over the shock of that now as I quite unexpectedly found I could do it myself! I also decided to do a refresher Alpha course last year and felt I got a lot more out of it that time around.

What has He done in my life? I'd like to say He's

made me a better person - although I often feel as if I'm falling short as a Christian - but I do pray regularly for help as well as praise so I have to trust I'm forgiven. He's made me feel grounded and so grateful for my life. As you will have gathered from the above I didn't suddenly see the light I've been very much a slow burn

Beccy

I became a disciple of Christ in 2003, although I would have regarded myself as a Christian before this.

It happened through attending Alpha run in our local church during a particularly difficult time in my life and it was during the prayer session I knew that Jesus was my saviour, that he had died for my sins and that he was always there for me through the good and hard times. After Alpha I found that I needed to move church for my faith to move forward and so I spent a number of years at a church in our local town. Just about the time that a new Rector arrived in the parish I was about to have my son and so then it seemed like a good time to return to the Parish.

Now I know he is always with me, I trust my life in him, I turn to him in difficult times and give thanks when he guides me - my prayer during testing times is - 'I believe and trust in him' this has helped me through very difficult times. There are still questions that I can't answer but I don't doubt he is with me.

Sarah

I was brought up as a Christian going to Sunday School and Church regularly. As an A level student of chemistry, botany and zoology, we had interesting discussions with our teacher about creation. Studying cells and atoms was so fascinating, I felt there had to be a God.

As an adult, I continued to go to church on Sunday and pray occasionally, probably when I had a list of needs. The challenge came in 1973 – on a Lent course in our local town. One of the questions was 'How are Christians different from those who are not?' Nobody could answer. Certainly no one was better than anyone else. Yes, we believed in God and they didn't but what difference did it make to us and our lives. The question troubled me. I began to wonder if there was any point. At the service that Easter Day, I kept being aware of the words of joy and excitement as we celebrated the resurrection. As I knelt at the altar rail, I thought if it was true we should actually be falling on our faces in total awe. I asked God then that if it was all true, I wanted to feel that awe and joy and would he make it very clear to me.

It was time to move. Three children and a dog living in the flat above the shop was getting too difficult. We found a house nearby. Just as we were about to exchange contracts the sellers, who had already moved out, decided they didn't want to sell after all and moved back in. They did at least pay all the expenses we had incurred (surveyor's and solicitor's fees). The next house, (a bungalow which we planned to extend), was tucked away across the road in the grounds of a large house. We were just about to exchange contracts again when the owner of the large house who was selling the bungalow asked us what we would do about the mains water which came through his garden in the winter. His garden taps were attached and he would be turning the water off to stop them freezing. We would have to install new mains from the road and up the drive – hugely expensive. We withdrew from the sale and we later learnt he had decided he wanted it for his mother. Two strange reasons for house sales to fall through. The next house was in M, a straightforward purchase. I continued worshipping in our local town. Until I received a courtesy visit from the Rector of the church in M. He invited me join his discussion group. It was open to anyone regardless of faith and included some with no faith trying to challenge him. They were studying John in the Authorised version. Literally verse by verse. They were near the end of the first chapter by the time I joined. It was fascinating. I had never studied the Bible like that before. Eventually we reached chapter 4 and the story of the woman at the well. Verse 26: 'I that speak to thee am HE.' It spoke directly to me. I felt He was right here with me NOW (not that I associated myself with the woman at the well!). Being born again suddenly made sense. Salvation and conviction of sin gradually followed.

Up until then I had forgotten my prayer and it

wasn't until a little while afterwards that I realised God's hand must have been in the failure of the first two house sales which led us to M. He had answered my prayer. A number of people came to faith in that group including some who thought they could prove otherwise.

I couldn't live without Jesus now. He has carried me and my family through some very difficult times and I never cease to be amazed at his love and his patience. He is still teaching me stuff and showing me things and helping me along the way and presenting me with challenges. And the pain and anguish that he went through for us still hits home. Needless to say, there are still times when I struggle in my own strength and forget to trust Him.